PRAISE FOR *STRENGTH IN WEAKNESS*

"Reading this amazing book, I was reminded of a citrus farmer who showed me how a tree becomes root-bound. The roots wind around and grow inward, actually strangling the tree. Andy untangles the roots of our most complex relationships and plants us firmly in the cross."

CAROL WIMBER

"With his characteristic candor and clarity, Andy Comiskey leads us through his own journey toward sexual completeness and spiritual wholeness. His theological insights regarding human sexuality and relational authenticity are biblically based and practically applied. There is a profound spiritual depth to this book that dares to recognize the toxic nature of sin in order to release the healing power of grace. As we experience healing and completeness as sexual persons, we discover wholeness and health as spiritual persons. Reading this book is to be led by the Good Shepherd beside still waters and discover the power of the One who 'restores my soul.'"

RAY S. ANDERSON, SENIOR PROFESSOR OF THEOLOGY AND MINISTRY, FULLER SEMINARY

"That strength can be found in my weaknesses is something I have always known but never fully understood. Using his deep spiritual insights and his wonderful gifts as a writer, Andy Comiskey has opened up my heart to the real meaning of this truth."

ALAN MEDINGER, AUTHOR OF *GROWTH INTO MANHOOD*

"In this honest book, Comiskey reveals that setbacks and temptations are inevitable stumbling blocks along the long, difficult road to gender wholeness. This is true for anyone seeking release from any deep-seated psychological condition or behavioral pattern—substance addiction, depression, feelings of worthlessness or the struggle against unwanted attractions. Yet it is often the wounded healers—when they are open about the frailty that often attends victory—who go on to live the boldest and most victorious lives. I highly recommend this book."

JOSEPH NICOLOSI, PH.D., PRESIDENT OF THE NATIONAL ASSOCIATION OF RESEARCH AND THERAPY OF HOMOSEXUALITY (NARTH)

"Comiskey shows how important it is for a man to be truly masculine and a woman to be truly feminine, and for each to complement the other. While sin destroys the harmony that ought to exist between man and woman, Christ rescues man and woman from isolation by becoming the bond between them, prompting each to be reconciled with the other."

REV. JOHN F. HARVEY, OSFS, DIRECTOR OF COURAGE

"Strength in Weakness makes it clear that what God gives to the weak really is strength and not weakness. We are enabled to be 'strong in the Lord, and in the power of his might,' as Paul said. And we can learn to negotiate the intricacies of fantasy, feeling and context in such a way that we do walk in holiness and power wherever we are. These are universal lessons of the way of Christ, no matter what one's personal history may be."

DALLAS WILLARD, PH.D.

STRENGTH
IN
Weakness

Overcoming Sexual and

Relational Brokenness

ANDREW COMISKEY

InterVarsity Press
Downers Grove, Illinois

InterVarsity Press
P.O. Box 1400, Downers Grove, IL 60515-1426
World Wide Web: www.ivpress.com
E-mail: mail@ivpress.com

InterVarsity Press® is the book-publishing division of InterVarsity Christian Fellowship/USA®, a student movement active on campus at hundreds of universities, colleges and schools of nursing in the United States of America, and a member movement of the International Fellowship of Evangelical Students. For information about local and regional activities, write Public Relations Dept., InterVarsity Christian Fellowship/USA, 6400 Schroeder Rd., P.O. Box 7895, Madison, WI 53707-7895, or visit the IVCF website at <www.ivcf.org>.

Cover design: Cindy Kiple

Cover and interior image: Bill Hatcher/National Geographic Society

ISBN 0-8308-2368-9

Printed in the United States of America ∞

Library of Congress Cataloging-in-Publication Data

Comiskey, Andrew.
   Strength in weakness: overcoming sexual and relational brokenness/
Andrew Comiskey.
     p. cm.
Includes bibliographical references.
   ISBN 0-8303-2368-9 (pbk.: alk. paper)
   1. Sex—Religious aspects—Christianity. 2.
   Homosexuality—Religious
aspects—Christianity. 3. Man-woman relationships—Religious
aspects—Christianity. I. Title.
   BT708.C655 2003
   241'.66—dc21
2003006795

P	18	17	16	15	14	13	12	11	10	9	8	7	6	5	4	3	2
Y	18	17	16	15	14	13	12	11	10	09	08	07	06	05	04	03

To my parents,

Phyllis and Tom Comiskey,

whose love and acceptance

freed me to admit my weakness

without shame.

And to

Leanne Payne and the late John Wimber,

whose commitment to making the church

a healing community

empowered me to do the same.

CONTENTS

ACKNOWLEDGMENTS

I want to thank Don Sciortino for pastoring me through this project and through a challenging season of church life. Don, your advocacy, warmth and wisdom helped me to see the bride with new eyes.

Thanks are also due to my faithful assistant, Mark Pertuit, for pressing through in order to help me complete this project. And to my editor, Cindy Bunch, for her guidance and patience. You both made this book a better one!

Thanks to my family—my wife, Annette, and kids, Greg, Nick, Katie and Sam. You are the fruit and reward of God's strength at work in my weakness. Bless you for putting up with my frailties (on vivid display at home over the course of my writing this book).

Introduction

My wife, Annette, and I recently celebrated our twentieth wedding anniversary. But that was not the only milestone we passed. We also celebrated the twentieth anniversary of the ministry we founded: Desert Stream. Through Desert Stream we and the other members of our team equip people to find healing in Christ for their sexual and relational brokenness.

To mark our marriage and ministry anniversaries, Annette and I spent nine days on vacation in New York City, enjoying the city's cultural treasures. I was particularly moved by some of the depictions of Christ on the cross that we encountered at art museums. These medieval and Renaissance works powerfully portrayed the way of deliverance that God has made for broken ones. Over and over these words of Bonaventure rang in my mind: "There is no other path but through the burning love of the Crucified."[1]

Furthermore, while we were in New York, Annette and I had time to reflect on how God had healed our own brokenness. I had been set free from homosexuality and my wife had recovered from the effects of childhood sexual abuse. It had not been easy for either of us, of course, but then good things rarely are. Now we felt secure in the love of God and the love we shared between us, which had resulted in the wonderful blessing of our four children. My sense of security, though, was about to be shaken.

Neither of us had spent much time in Manhattan prior to our vacation, and now we were taken aback by the pervasiveness of homosexuality in the culture. As we walked the streets, it seemed that at every turn we met gay men who were intent on engaging with us and were wondering whether Annette and I were a couple. It all had a troubling effect on me.

The assertiveness of the homosexuals we encountered caused me to work harder to assert who I was and what I stood for, and that was good. But at the same time—I have to admit it—these overtures were appealing to me. Against the sophisticated backdrop of Manhattan, the homosexual lifestyle appeared highly seductive.

Thankfully I soon came to my senses. It happened as Annette and I were walking in Greenwich Village, just across the street from the site of the Stonewall riots—the official starting point for the gay rights movement in America. Nearby was a park featuring sculptures of two same-sex couples. We couldn't take it any more. We prayed together, asserting our true identities in Christ and calling on him to reclaim lives in the Village.

As if in confirmation of our intent to honor Christ, he honored us with a chance to minister to someone who was needy.

While wending our way through the Village, we met a woman with whom we felt compelled to share about Jesus Christ and his love. A lapsed Catholic, she hungrily received our words and exclaimed in tears how we were an answer to her prayers. Just two hours earlier she had asked God for guidance. Apparently we were her counselors that day, directing her to Christ.

STRENGTH IN WEAKNESS: DO YOU SEE IT?

I have discovered that God does not free me from all of my weaknesses. Rather, he frees me to cry out to him as I struggle to do what is right. Then he is faithful to release his power again and again and again.

When submitted to God, our weaknesses have holy purposes. They challenge the limitations of our self-reliance. And they remind us—more often than we would like—of our need for the greater strength God can provide.

WEAKNESS IN SERVICE TO CHRIST

The apostle Paul proclaimed God's strength in his weakness. It happened when the Corinthians accused him of being unimpressive (2 Cor 10:1—11:15). How did Paul defend himself? By boasting of his accomplishments? No. He defended his apostolic call with a single remarkable theme: strength in weakness. "If I must boast," he wrote, "I will boast of the things that show my weakness" (11:30).

Paul resorted to the cross as his basis for understanding strength in weakness. He had grasped the truth that crucifixion precedes resurrection, first for Christ and then for us as Christ's followers. As he wrote in 2 Corinthians 13:4, "[Jesus] was crucified in weakness, yet he lives by God's power. Likewise, we are weak in him, yet by God's power we will live with him to serve you."

Weakness in service to Christ? Any Christian worker knows that the pressure of ministry can cause certain weaknesses to surface, even those weaknesses we may have thought we had mastered. I experienced one such weakness—and the power of God at work through it—during a conference on sexual wholeness held several years ago.

I returned to my hotel room one evening and discovered that for some reason my television was receiving the "adult" channel even though I had not paid for it. I was shocked. And I was curious. Several years had passed since I had been exposed to pornography. What would it be like to watch such images now?

The images drew me and damned me at the same time. I watched for a few moments, then tried to fight back by calling the hotel desk as well as Annette and my prayer partners. But the hotel clerk said he was not able to turn off the channel, and no one else was home when I called. Thwarted on all fronts, I decided to watch the sexual images some more. Though little time had elapsed, my brain was now ignited.

Blessedly, just then the phone rang—it was a return call from a friend. I confessed my sin and we prayed for God to forgive me. But more than that, we prayed for God to strengthen me in my weakness.

After the phone call, I knew I could not go near the television set, so I lay down to sleep in the bathroom. For a long time, though, sleep would not come. A voice in my mind accused me, *How can you lead others to freedom when you are so weak?* I looked at myself, the mighty healer, huddled next to the toilet. It was pathetic. So I resolved to tell my host (a pastor) that I could not speak at his church the next morning due to my sin and weakness.

I thought then that I would have peace and be able to fall asleep. But God challenged me on my resolution. I believed I could hear him telling me, "Andy, your struggle is what qualifies you to serve." It seemed he wanted me to go ahead and speak the next day even though, or even *because,* I am weak before temptation just like everybody else.

The next morning I told the whole story to the pastor. He affirmed my qualification to speak. And let me tell you, that morning the Lord moved with unprecedented power to release many from shame and impurity. His mercy poured from this weak and weary vessel!

LAYERS AROUND WEAKNESS

Before proceeding to look at the nature of Paul's weakness, it may be helpful for us to look at the various layers that can surround weakness. In so doing I will use my struggle to break free from pornography as an example. Looking at the layers that obscure our weakness—whatever it may be—can free us to face the real problem more effectively.

First, we face *shame* in the struggle. That means we tend to feel bad about the problem, even to the extent that we want to hide it. Like Adam and Eve in the garden, we cover ourselves with fig leaves.

We pretend we are fine even though we know we are not.

That night in the hotel, with pornography filling my TV screen, I could have chosen not to call anyone. And the next day I could have hypocritically powered through the sermon I had prepared. That's what shame does. It silences us. It causes us to lie and to rely on ourselves.

Second, underneath the shame, God mercifully exposes the next layer—our *sin*. No matter how out of control we feel in our compulsion, the truth is that we are making choices. We thus contribute to our estrangement from God and others; we make decisions that damage our key relationships.

This is not weakness but wickedness. God wants to forgive, but he can do that only if we acknowledge the sin that stems from our weakness. Having received forgiveness, we are then free to receive holy power where we need it the most.

It's true I was surprised by the pornographic images coming from my television set. And yet I could have turned off the television when I saw what it was—*but I didn't.* I watched for a while, and then when my first attempts to change the situation failed, I watched some more. I *chose* to watch. That was my sin.

Another layer is our *wounding*. Such wounding may be physical abuse or inadequate love and affirmation or any number of other harmful effects. These wounds contribute to our misdirected grasping after love, fueling our sin.

For me, rejection early in my life set me on the road toward sexual confusion and an unwise search for love. In that way my wounding made me susceptible to the pull of pornography.

At the core, once the layers of shame, sin and wounding have been peeled away, lies our *weakness*. This weakness includes the tendency toward habitual sin. This tendency is not in itself sin, nor need it be shrouded by shame or empowered by unhealed wounds, but it does lead to many problems.

One of my weaknesses is a compulsion to look at illicit images.

Now, God has given me much grace and power to free me from this compulsion, and I thank God for that. But the weakness remains.

Of course, I am not always mindful of it. As a matter of fact, the temptation has decreased to the extent that at times I feel completely free of it—that is, until I am faced once more by the emergence of that tendency. Then I have a choice: to submit to the world of false pleasure or to submit to God and trustworthy others. Therein lies his ability to strengthen me.

Our weaknesses, then, can be distinguished from our shame, our sin and our wounds. We will be exploring all three in the chapters to come. Our goal? To surrender our weaknesses to God and others so that, like Paul, we might discover God's strength as we seek to serve him in our weaknesses.

NAMING THE THORN

What was Paul's weakness? Described by Paul as a "thorn in my flesh" (2 Cor 12:7), this weakness was something in him that was flawed or fragile, not whole. The weakness did not conform to Paul's idea of how he should be. The enemy even had access to "torment" him through that weakness. God did not remove that weakness even though Paul pleaded with him to do so (v. 8). God had other plans for the thorn—he desired to use it to anchor the apostle in divine grace and power.

We are not sure of the nature of Paul's weakness; many alternatives have been suggested. Regardless, we can identify our weakness with his. And we can receive the very words that the Lord spoke to Paul in response to the apostle's prayer for deliverance from his weakness: "My grace is sufficient for you, for my power is made perfect in weakness" (2 Cor 12:9).

Let's break down that response. Rather than freeing Paul from his weakness, God offered the apostle his grace. And God claimed that his power would become most apparent in Paul through the weakened area of his humanity. The word translated "perfect" connotes a full maturity. God's strength would come to fruition in the fertile ground of Paul's weakness.

The apostle grasped clearly throughout his ministry how well suited his weakness was to receive and bear divine power. One commentator declared, "The startling contrast between the two [only served] . . . to magnify the superabundance of [God's] sufficiency."[2] Paul's weakness revealed God's power more clearly than did his gifts and strengths.

Just as the lower end of a dry valley drinks in the rain most deeply, so the cavities of Paul's soul received the outpouring of God's Spirit. He followed Jesus, who endured the weakness of the cross for the glorious power of the resurrection. Standing in Christ's example, Paul allowed his weaknesses to reveal God's strength through him.

BEFRIENDING OUR WEAKNESS

Paul's second letter to the Corinthians is a valentine to human weakness. Through that letter the apostle implores us to befriend our frailties, for then we can act in God's power.

The cross guided Paul into that realization. Christ, weak in his dying, was empowered in his rising. We, in turn, are weak, yet we are made strong in our yielding to Christ. He raises us up to love well, not in spite of our weaknesses but in and through them.

From the outset of our relationship, Annette would accompany me to our healing meetings in West Hollywood. At first she resented the depth of brokenness we saw in some of the people to whom we ministered. She felt that more normal and resilient ones, like herself, might be more deserving of grace, at least the grace she had to give.

At one of the meetings, though, God challenged her. During a group prayer time, he called her to lay down her judgments—to surrender how she saw and felt about the group members.

As the prayer was closing, Annette looked around the room and saw the members with new eyes. God inspired Annette with fresh vision and compassion for the group. Following Christ's example, she "died," and in her dying the Father released a fountain of his mercy in her. Out of her weakness he empowered Annette with holy love, which flows from her to this day.

God supplies his strength for our weakness in many ways. In this book I want to look at how God takes the weaknesses we experience in our relationships and in our sexuality and uses them to establish his powerful love in us. In those areas where we fail to love well, God meets us and invites us into a deeper communion with himself.

God also invites us to join with others so that our empowering can become established in context with real people. While God pervades the process of gaining strength in weakness, he is not content for it to be a string of lonely mystical experiences. He wants to use other people to empower us to love well. I pray that this book will help you toward that end.

1

GOD'S IMAGE IN HUMANITY

Sonja's childhood in Germany was spoiled by abuse of various kinds, while her teenage years and young adult life were marked by addiction to alcohol, pornography and sexual fantasy. Her early wounding predisposed her to believe that no one, especially men, would ever care for her. She thus sought to meet her own needs through drugs and fantasy. Such responses, in turn, led to shame and self-hatred.

Her affliction intensified when she was excommunicated from her church due to her struggle with sexual fantasies for certain men in the congregation. Sonja had never acted on these desires; still, she was deemed a threat. Abandoned by the church, she also felt abandoned by God. Ultimately she was restored to fellowship, but her heart remained broken in its capacity to trust God and the kindness of his people.

She arrived at Desert Stream Ministries in great need of the healing for sexual and relational brokenness we help supply. Slowly she began to open up to us. Through the prayers of caring believers, she discovered God's comfort as well as cleansing from her sin. His power began to replace the shame that previously had covered her vulnerabilities.

Especially helpful for Sonja was the love of the men on staff. Because of her history of abuse, most of which came from men, Sonja had yet to really trust men. She either hated them or fantasized about them from a distance. The pure respect and affection she received from the Desert Stream men further enabled her to receive love. She could then refuse both her illusions and her defensive self-sufficiency toward men.

Her growth continued over her five years with us. Sonja has since returned to Europe, where she coordinates the ministry of Living Waters—our healing, teaching and discipleship series—for the entire continent.

Sonja's gifting to reach Europe became apparent during our first conference in Paris. Many had gathered to receive healing in areas of sexual and relational brokenness. They responded hungrily to the stories and teachings shared by all the speakers. However, it was not until Sonja spoke that the power of the Holy Spirit broke through.

Her starting point was strength in weakness, physically speaking, as she was sick with the flu at the time. She haltingly stepped up to speak, then shared her history of abuse and addiction, the shame that pervaded it all and the slow but sure breakthrough of God's grace. In all this the apostle Paul's self-description could be applied to her. She "did not come with eloquence or superior wisdom." She "came . . . in weakness and fear, and with much trembling . . . but with a demonstration of the Spirit's power, so that [their] faith might not rest on men's wisdom, but on God's power" (1 Cor 2:1-5).

As Sonja spoke to the French gathered for the conference, her words pierced their hearts. People responded en masse to release their shame to Jesus so that he could cover their affliction with his powerful grace. The Spirit administered that truth mightily through a weak vessel, yet one containing the power of God.

Sonja exemplifies how God empowers us to love others well. And loving well really matters to God because he created us to be in right relationship with others.

Indeed God commands us to work out our humanity and our salvation together as male and female. Doing so exposes our sin—and a slew of weaknesses underlying our sin. But given the truth of who God calls us to be, we can honestly admit where we are not yet what we ought to be. We can then welcome God's strength into our relational weakness.

JESUS AND THE TRUE SELF

We need holy ground on which to stand and relate to one another, and that ground is our identification with Jesus Christ. His offer of resurrection raises us up so that we can approach one another with new vision and new life. As Pope John Paul II wrote, "When the human heart enters an alliance with this ethos, . . . the deepest and yet most real possibilities and dispositions of the person are manifested."[1] Jesus alone possesses the love that can call forth our true design from the darkness that has shrouded it.

Suppose a painter created a beautiful painting, one that bore his distinctive style. His pride in the painting was matched only by his distress when it fell into the hands of vandals who mistreated the painting until its original design was barely recognizable. Their fingerprints smudged it; layers of dust and grime obscured the painting's true form and colors. The artist searched everywhere, going from gallery to loft to attic until he found his work. Then gently, with unerring accuracy and skill, he restored the work, repairing the damage and enabling his design to emerge.

Jesus is that master painter. He persists in love in order to reclaim the true self in each of us. Then we, through the power of his love, begin to emerge as we in truth are. This has profound implications for our personal identities and our relationships.

The biblical creation story provides the basis for understanding authentic personhood and relationships. Genesis 1—2 shows us our true design as male and female together. Genesis 3 provides the keys to how and why we became broken. The sources of our sin and shame, including the hostility between the sexes, lie there.

But while the creation story tells us how we got in this shape, hope for recovery of our true identity is anchored in our union with Jesus. His cross, in fact, is the lens through which we can view both God's design for humanity and its brokenness. Every barrier in us becomes Christ's opportunity.

For some, beholding the damage done to humanity creates a temptation to despair. If that is the case for you, look up! Christ has broken the chains that shackle our efforts to love. And he pours out his power to enable even the weakest of us to love well.

In other words, we go through Christ to get to Adam. While the original pair—Adam and Eve—provide keys to God's intention for our own humanity, especially in the areas of gender and sexuality, Christ alone is the means to authenticating that intention in our lives. What the Father wills for us, Jesus enables us to realize through his strength at work in our weakness.

MADE IN GOD'S IMAGE

God's intentions for humanity are summarized by the declaration that "God created man in his own image" (Gen 1:27). Somehow we reflect him in a way that makes us different from any other created being.

Our bearing God's image means that we represent him. And a crucial part of this representation involves our having an upright relationship with him. How can one reflect light unless he or she is in a position to receive its rays?

Genesis 1, offering the first version of God's creation of Adam and Eve, shows that they were upright before the Creator. These two stood in unqualified communion with him. Indeed I believe that worship of God was their primary identity and function—authentic worship confirmed their authentic humanity.

As one expression of their devotion, the pair had the authority to rule over the earth (1:28). Rightfully submitted to God's reign, these human bearers of his image reigned with him over the rest of creation.

What is crucial for our purposes is that God's image is revealed in dual form: humanity as male and female. Genesis 1 describes image bearing as a relationship between two human beings.

God created man in his own image,
in the image of God he created him;
male and female he created them. (1:27)

Adam and Eve required more than union with God in order to know their true selves; they were created to know each other as well.

It is not too much to say that Genesis 1:26-27 provides the thesis statement for a high and holy view of men and women standing together before their Creator, united in relationship and in mission. Their service extends to one another as they represent God's powerful provision of love to the other. As Donald Bloesch wrote, "We find our humanity only by losing ourselves in the service of the welfare of our fellow humanity, who always exists in twofold form: male and female."[2] John Paul II extended this view by saying, "Man can fully discover his true self only in a sincere giving of himself."[3]

The bearing of God's image, then, involves two things for humanity: an upright relationship with the Creator and a commitment to relating to his fellow image bearers. The second creation account, contained in Genesis 2, helps us understand the implications of all this better.

MALE AND FEMALE

The creation account in Genesis 2 elaborates on the yearning for relationship that God instilled in his still-sinless human creation. Here we read how God declared that the man was ill suited to stand by himself. "I will make a helper suitable for him," determined the Creator (v. 18). Then he went on to form Eve from Adam's rib. The two met, drawn by their suitability for each other and yearning for their original unity.

While God created Adam and Eve both as bearers of his image, their meeting together authenticated that call. In other words, the two discovered their inspired humanity in union with each other. As John Paul II wrote, "Man becomes the image of God not so much in the moment of solitude as in the moment of communion."[4]

We cannot discount nor downplay that call upon the original couple to become human in the rich exchange between the two of them. Though his humanity was determined by God, said Ray Anderson, "Adam cannot be complete without encountering himself in the other who is 'bone of his bone and flesh of his flesh.' "[5] His humanity hinged at once upon his communion with God and his communion with the woman.

Part of God's provision for Adam and Eve's humanity lay in their difference. Likewise, we are rightfully called out of our aloneness by the blend of similarity and dissimilarity that marks heterosexual encounter. As Anderson remarked, "Intimacy is intensified by otherness."[6] How can one's aloneness be eased, his or her humanity rounded out, unless that person encounters members of the opposite sex in their inspired difference?

The dance of difference between man and woman is in truth inspired. Its purpose? For the two parts to create a whole, thereby representing God in his fullness on the face of the earth.

Though Genesis 2 grants us few clues into the intrinsic difference between man and woman, one significant variance can be gleaned from the different forms of their creation. God formed the man "from the dust of the ground" (v. 7). This predisposed the man toward a special relationship with the soil; he would tend to be more identified with the work of his hands than would be the woman. She, on the other hand, was taken from the man (vv. 21-22). Eve was thus inclined to define herself more in terms of her relationships. We could say that her greater strength lay in her capacity to be for others, while the man's greater strength lay in his doing.

These inclinations emerged out of creation and were free from particular role prescriptions. Before the Lord, both the man and the woman possessed a freedom for spiritual devotion and relational harmony. Their posture was upright before the Lord and each was secure in the love of the other. Together they bore the image as equal and yet different counterparts in God's whole intention for humanity.

In paradise the power struggles now common to male-female relationships did not exist. There Adam and Eve complemented one another in a way that revealed the best of each. I believe Adam, in his greater physical strength, loved Eve powerfully, encircling her softness in his desire to secure her in love. And Eve, in her more feeling heart, responded to his strength with powerful love—a love that awakened his heart and satisfied the emptiness within.

Their differences united them. In paradise they discovered wholeness, not a striving for power. Paul alluded to this interdependence when he said, "In the Lord . . . woman is not independent of man, nor is man independent of woman. For as woman came from man, so also man is born of woman. But everything comes from God" (1 Cor 11:11-12).

GENDER MATTERS

God's intention for humanity is represented by the harmony of man and woman together. But that freedom to be for another requires security in one's personal identity as male or female. Thus gender security matters profoundly.

In paradise that security was a given. But in the post-garden reality of a child's development, one can either grow or fail to grow into that confident posture. Whereas biology determines one's physical sex, gender identity involves the more complex process of acquiring a sense of oneself as male or female. And that process can go wrong.

Still, it remains true that security in one's own identity as a man or a woman precedes the freedom to be for another. The compelling nature of the "otherness" perceived in a member of the opposite sex results from the clarity and security one experiences in his or her own gender identity.[7]

The image of God, then, involves gender identity *and* complementarity. God created gender in its duality as male and female. And he created us as his representatives to discover that duality. In order to be true to the divine command, a person must reckon forthrightly and concretely with his maleness or her femaleness in relation to the other.

The "true self" always includes one's gender identity and its relation to the opposite sex. We live in an age when many speak in hushed tones about gender differences for fear of sounding sexist. For the sake of truth, however, we must hold fast to gender identity and complementarity as central to the image of God.

John Paul II spoke profoundly to the power God's image when he said that the "dignity and balance [of human life] depend . . . on who she will be for him, and he for her."[8] The harmony of man and woman together engenders security in the lives that emerge out of that union. Generations are blessed by the respectful, committed love between a man and a woman.

Karl Barth laid out three basic points that govern the outworking of this dignifying interdependence between man and woman.

First, one must be faithful to God by standing in one's own gender. That means discovering the clarity and security we need to stand uprightly as ourselves in regard to the opposite sex. We find our distinctly masculine or feminine voice and in gratitude go forward to exercise it in relation to the other gender. Barth wrote, "The essential point is that woman must always and in all circumstances be woman: that she must feel and conduct herself as such and not as man. . . . The command of the Lord . . . directs both the man and the woman to their own proper sacred place and forbids all attempts to violate that order."[9]

This increasing clarity and ease in one's gender issues forth from God's command to be male or female. Barth implored people to be not merely aware of their gender, "but honestly glad of it, thanking God that they are allowed to be members of their particular sex and therefore soberly and with good conscience going the way marked out for them in this distinctive."[10]

Second, we are to go forward in our gender distinctive and engage with the opposite sex. "There is no such thing as a self-contained and self-sufficient male or female life," said Barth.[11] One lives out the divine command by "remaining true to this polar relationship, ripe for it and active to it."[12]

While gender security precedes wholeness in heterosexual relating, it is also strengthened by such relating. One is empowered in his or her own gender by actively engaging with the other. "The male is a male in the Lord . . . to the extent that he is with the female, and the female likewise." Barth insisted that such engaging be worked out in reality and not merely be assented to.[13]

Third, true complementarity involves masculine initiative and feminine response. Barth cited the special responsibility of the one who was created first. In humility before God, man takes "the lead as the inspirer, leader, and initiator in their common being and action." But of course this order "would have no meaning if [the woman] did not follow and occupy her own place in it."[14]

Part of man's greater tendency to do and to act involves his initiating with woman. Her response imbues the relationship with heart. He instigates, but she is catalytic in the union due to her more developed relational sensibility.

That in no way means that men alone initiate and women only respond. Over the course of their relating together, both genders interact with a variety of initiatives and responses. Still, there exists an essential rhythm of masculine initiative and feminine response that helps secure both parties in the goodness of their genders.

Man needs to act lovingly toward woman and to be blessed for it. She, in turn, needs to feel security in his love and to offer her heart to him. The command of God establishes a divine interdependence between man and woman that lends balance and dignity to the two as well as to those around them.

IMAGE BEARING APPLIES TO ALL

It may sound as though I am referring primarily, if not exclusively, to marriage. Though I will talk about the marital covenant as one expression of God's image, I want to make it clear beforehand that single people bear the image as fully as do married people. All are called by God to work out their distinctiveness as one gender in relation to the other. In that interaction we discover the provision of God for our aloneness and the practical need for what the other imparts that we do not possess.

Perhaps we as a culture have so emphasized the sexual dimension of maleness and femaleness that we have lost sight of the power of friendship between men and women. We need each other. Many will not forge a marriage covenant, but all must obey God's command to live interdependently with the opposite gender. One can become a good gift to the other without romantic intentions or practice.

Marriage does not qualify one as a bearer of the divine image; God does. He commands unmarried and married persons alike to engage with members of the opposite sex. In so doing, we exercise our humanity and more fully reveal the image of God in us. "Unmarried persons . . . are not denied full completion of the imago dei," wrote Anderson.[15] And Barth declared, "Whether in love or marriage or outside this bond, every woman and every man should realize that he is committed to live consciously and willingly in this interrelationship, not regarding his own being abstractly as his own but as being in fellowship and shaping it accordingly."[16]

But what about the specifically sexual dimension of our humanity? We experience the bodily urge to merge with a member of the opposite sex physically. How does that urge relate to our nature as bearers of God's image?

SEXUALITY AND THE IMAGE OF GOD

The first thing to note about sexual desire is that God inspired that longing in us when he called us to be human, to bear his image as male and female. Indeed sexual desire emerges out of gender complementarity. What better reveals the difference between the sexes than the longing of the man to enter into the woman and the woman's desire to receive him?

We catch a glimpse of that longing for union in Genesis 2. God removed Adam's rib and reshaped it into the woman. Both now possessed an aspect of the other; each was whole and yet longed for communion with the missing part. That's why Adam declared of his wife,

> This is now bone of my bones
> and flesh of my flesh;
> she shall be called "woman,"
> for she was taken out of man. (v. 23)

The longing of the two for their original state of union distilled the essence of sexual desire. It was a gift from God, as it emerged out of his creative intention for humanity.

In paradise, consequently, we glimpse the formation of marriage. "A man will leave his father and mother and be united to his wife, and they will become one flesh" (v. 24). The sexual act sealed Adam and Eve's reunion. It symbolized their oneness and satisfied their aloneness.

Such is the power of sexual intercourse. It makes us one with another for life. Though we continue to live as male or female with many others, sex renders the marital relationship exclusive. When we marry someone and consummate that marriage with intercourse, we declare a unique oneness with this other. Until parted by death, this one will be primary, and therefore others secondary, in the working out of our humanity on earth, before God, as male and female.

Yet in order for intercourse to be constructive, it must be preceded by a conscious commitment to unite with the other on levels less binding than the physical. We first must seek to know this other with our clothes on, revealing who we are on emotional, intellectual and spiritual levels. We can then determine if in truth this is the one with whom we will choose to share an exclusive lifetime bond. Only when two persons are ready to do the hard work of forging a lifelong commitment are they ready to become one flesh.

The intimate power of intercourse functions as the signature on the contract. Sex may deepen intimacy, but it is only inspired to the degree that the one is committed to the other in the totality of his or her being. Barth wrote, "The Christian will realize that he can only enter into sexual relationship with her if each is concerned for the whole being of the other, so that for both of them it is not a question of something partial or future, as in prostitution, but . . . as something total."[17]

One is ready to be naked and unashamed before his or her desired partner (see Gen 2:25) only when committed in full to the other. Such commitment prepares the marriage bed. There the one-flesh union begins, only to be repeated over the course of a lifetime. Godly sex reminds both partners of their unity; it reinforces again and again the self-giving essential to finding oneself. We give the most powerful and precious offering of the self to the other. We then find ourselves, that lost part removed from us at creation.

But not only does godly sex require the boundaries of a lifetime commitment; so does the new life that is conceived in such a commitment. God commanded the first man and woman to "be fruitful and multiply" (Gen 1:28 NASB). Children resulted from their unity. Similarly, today, in order for parents-to-be to fulfill God's call responsibly, they must take seriously the need to provide a secure context for the raising of new life. The dignity and honor of children depend on it.

This parental commitment, furthermore, manifests with clarity the image of God as male and female. Through the presence of both parents, said John Paul II, children witness "the mystery of femininity [which] is manifested and revealed completely by means of motherhood. . . . Man's masculinity, that is, the generative and fatherly meaning of his body, is also thoroughly revealed."[18]

God makes it clear that his image bearers must live in dynamic communion with one another, thereby discovering and celebrating the good gift of one's own gender and that of the other. With a cross-shaped lens, we behold the beauty of man for woman and woman for man. None of us has ever lost that original design. No matter how broken we have become, we have never lost the potential to be good gifts for others!

2

FACING THE BROKEN IMAGE

Glen and Greg seemed worlds apart. A gay activist, Glen was driven by anger toward the church or anyone whose truth threatened his homosexuality.

On the other hand, Greg was all smiles, a congenial Pentecostal minister who seemingly embraced the very truth that enraged Glen. But Greg's commitment to truth did not bar him from a profound addiction to pornography. His sin ate away at his marriage and the holy image he sought to project as a pastor.

God revealed his mercy to both men and freed them to face their brokenness. For Glen, this mercy began to break into his life when he and his fellow activists targeted a church in London that sponsored Living Waters. They disrupted the Sunday service there two weeks in a row, angrily and noisily protesting what they perceived to be that church's hatred of homosexuals.

The church responded in love, a gentle grace that challenged Glen's assumptions. A few months later, he returned to the church in a personal quest for that love. That love invited him to look at the real brokenness in his life. He attended the Living Waters program, where he found the support necessary to lay down his gay identity and find out the truth of how God saw him. He is now a happily married husband and father.

Greg needed to lay down a false identity as well. He needed the grace to forsake his projected image of wholeness and face how broken he really was. Through a counselor, then a men's support group, Greg dared to accept that he as a leader was also a sinner capable of deception and destruction. He had to ask himself honestly, *What matters more to me—real wholeness or the appearance of it?*

For both men, freedom to live out God's design for their life involved an honest look at how broken they truly were. It is the same for us. Only in dealing honestly with the shame, sin and wounding that shroud God's image in us can we begin to emerge out of our brokenness. The original masterpiece longs to be unveiled. With Jesus as our guide, we dare to peel away the layers that obscure the true design. That is key to becoming good gifts for others, strengthened in our weakness to love well.

God called Adam and Eve to care for the garden together. The one condition of their reign was that they not partake of the tree of the knowledge of good and evil (Gen 2:16-17). Their freedom depended on their living without the fruit of that tree. But disobedience enslaved their freedom to love.

THE HIDDENNESS OF SIN

The pair's refusal to obey God became the basis for the broken image, the tendency fallen humanity possesses to act unnaturally. Sin wars against our native desire and capacity to uprightly love God and others. Anderson wrote, "Disobedience . . . is therefore a denial of one's own humanity. . . . To live in such a way as to resist the Word and will of God in favor of our instinctive rights and desires is to live inhumanly."[1]

While obedience frees people to be good gifts to God and others, sin demands concealment. The third chapter of Genesis clearly describes the effects of sin upon the image bearers. First, Adam and Eve sought to hide from each other by clothing themselves (Gen 3:7). No longer unashamed, they covered their genitals so as to conceal themselves from each other.

The fig leaf conveyed shame and separation from pure trust in the other's love. For the first time, each was self-conscious and uncertain of his or her identity in relation to the other. They were also conscious of the other's uncertainty. Responding to the other became risky. Each experienced the threat of his or her need for the other. Adam and Eve were then capable of exercising more than love—they could withhold love and deceive and damage one another.

Not surprisingly, the two also hid from God (Gen 3:8). Having disobeyed, they took matters into their own hands and fled the threat of exposure and punishment. The potential for separation from the Creator was conceived, and humanity ever since has borne its deadly consequences.

What a contrast this was to the couple's former peaceful reliance upon God! In paradise their unfettered devotion to God and each other rendered them secure in love. Their posture was one of openness and trust, toward God and one another. Disobedience disrupted this childlike reliance upon love. Fallen humanity fled from intimacy with God and the other and became self-protective.

It's no different with us. As descendants of the fallen pair, we too live antagonistically toward our Source and one another. John Paul II declared, "Without the freedom to be for God and the other, we live in contradiction to our basic humanity."[2] We no longer live in a relationship of openness and trust with God and one another. We sin and we hide in our shame. The armored and alienated selves we have become alienate others.

This cycle of alienation marks the broken image in humanity. We continue to bear God's image, but sin conceals it. Our inheritance of sin renders humanity capable of evil and of the good still contained in the broken image.

Following Eve's admission of how the serpent had deceived her with the forbidden fruit (Gen 3:13), God revealed the specific consequences of sin, beginning with the serpent. God cursed this creature. Assuming that the snake symbolizes Satan, we discover that one consequence of sin is prolonged spiritual hostility between the evil one and humanity.

> I [God] will put enmity
> > between you and the woman,
> > and between your offspring and hers;
> he will crush your head,
> > and you will strike his heel. (v. 15)

I will refer to the significance of the one who will crush the serpent's head later. For now I want to look at the power God granted the enemy to harass humanity.

The snake will strike at our heels. That conveys well Satan's authority to target vulnerable areas of our humanity and to undercut us there. His authority is not absolute; he cannot crush us. But he can antagonize us in areas of weakness.

To be more specific, these areas of weakness include the consequences of sin that God revealed to the first man and woman. These consequences would have a profound impact on how the two would relate to one another after the Fall.

ROOTS OF RELATIONAL BROKENNESS

After cursing the serpent, God cursed the woman and the man for their part in the disobedience. He said the woman would now be subject to an increase of pain in childbearing (Gen 3:16). But of greater import for our purposes is the second part of that verse:

> Your desire will be for your husband,
> > and he will rule over you.

What we see here is a divine pronouncement upon the nature of woman's desire for man after the Fall. But specifically what does that mean?

We have observed already how Eve was created from Adam and how this form of creation signaled a greater relational sensibility in

35

her. Though the first two chapters of Genesis tell us little about the precise nature of this sensibility, we can assume that Eve possessed a profound capacity to be in relationship with others. Furthermore, taken from Adam, Eve returned to him as one suited to come alongside him (2:18).

Eve was God's response to Adam's aloneness. And in fact, it was Eve's inspired response to him that awakened his heart. Adam, having been created first, yet languishing in his aloneness, became alive through her greater relational gift. But after the Fall, the woman's primary relational gift became a potential source of brokenness—all through her "desire" for him.

The word for "desire" in Genesis 3:16 can mean many things.[3] Perhaps the best interpretation is one that conveys inordinate desire, an exclusive, possessive yearning for the man. What distinguishes this desire from the life-giving freedom to be joined with him is its potentially compulsive quality. Under the weight of sin, woman loses a certain freedom to be in relationship with man. Instead she becomes insecure, grasping for meaning and purpose in union with him.

Woman's uprightness before God and man changed in the Fall. Now she desired man in a manner that threatened to become idolatrous. She bent toward him, seeking from him what he might not be capable of giving. Further, her greater relational strength, if detached from the security and strength of her identity in union with the Creator, set her up to bear the extra weight of his brokenness. In her heightened vulnerability toward man, she may become subject to broken expressions of manhood that damage her all the more.

Why, then, did God give her this "desire" as a consequence of her sin? Though vulnerable to the effects of brokenness in man, woman also is vulnerable to acting deceptively apart from him. In Genesis 3 we witness Eve's capacity to act independently of Adam in a manner that was destructive. She became persuaded by evil, and her husband followed suit (Gen 3:6). With the advent of sin, she became subject to his authority as a consequence and as a check to her potential for deception.

But Adam's rule over Eve resulted as much from his abdication of responsibility as it did from her initial deception. Although she led the way into sin, he willingly followed. Possessing the initial knowledge of the prohibition before the creation of woman (2:16-17), he said nothing to her about it. And when asked by her to partake of the fruit, he did. When interrogated by God, Adam even blamed the woman for the Fall—a cheap shot, given his knowledge and compliance. He abdicated his power to assert the truth where it was most needed in relation to his wife. He was thus commanded to rule over her as a consequence of his sloppy and immature response to her initial deception.

Man was created first and woman second. This order signifies something about man's need to initiate good for the woman and woman's need to respond to that good. In paradise such an order precluded the need for gender roles per se. Upright before God, both the man and the woman were free to thrive with God and each other without prescriptions of power. But in the Fall, woman was deceived first and led the man to deception—an act that inverted the gender order established at creation. This resulted in the hard consequence of Genesis 3:16, which established male leadership and female submission.

The consequence of sin for the man continues in 3:17-19. Not only did he now have to rule over the woman, but also the labor of his hands was now cursed. That's because his relation to the source of his creation—the earth—was twisted by sin and its consequence. (This parallels the damage inflicted on Eve's relationality, which derived from her creation from Adam's rib.)

Cursed is the ground because of you;
through painful toil you will eat of it
all the days of your life. (Gen 3:17)

The man was now vexed by the source of his creation, the earth, relating in a troubled fashion with it. His greater ability to act and to do, his inherent outer-directedness, turned on him in the Fall. He now lived painfully through the work of his hands. His punishment was tied to unrelenting labor:

> By the sweat of your brow
>   you will eat your food
> until you return to the ground,
>   since from it you were taken;
> for dust you are
>   and to dust you will return. (v. 19)

Because of Adam, man now faces a potentially idolatrous relationship with his work, as he is tempted to find his identity in his accomplishments. And this has implications for his relationship with woman. An addiction to accomplishment can rob him of becoming a gift to her. Further, his striving could support the myth that he, in his greater capacity to act, is in fact superior to the woman.

Bound to his work and ruling over the woman, man loses connection with his heart. He loses connection as well with the one whom God created to be a primary source of his own connectedness with others. Under the Fall, man struggles to love powerfully and well.

How far both Adam and Eve fell from the noble call to reign with God as his image bearers! Sin robbed them of key freedoms—the freedom to reign with God over the rest of creation and the freedom to enjoy one another, naked and unashamed. And they lost the freedom of intimacy with the Father, that unfettered communion with pure goodness. But that's not all—death was the most obvious and pronounced result of their sin (Gen 2:17; 3:22).

Before that end, however, sin and its deadly consequences would exact a heavy toll on the first couple's freedom to love God and to rejoice in the provision of the other. The two were cast out of the garden, ending the third chapter of Genesis.

POWER PLAYS

The Fall impacted the relationship between Adam and Eve in a way that we replay in our own lives today. Sin challenges inspired complementarity. Subject now to the effects of evil, men and women are capable of bruising each other. Our respective strengths—woman's relational sensibility, man's power to act—threaten to create discord rather than the wholeness God intended.

Heterosexual union remains God's intention for humanity. However, gender order is now subject to a kind of futility and brokenness. The two genders who in paradise revealed the Creator in their fullness as one flesh—mutuality and difference—now are subject to various relational disorders. We wound each other, and as we do so, our fig leaves thicken and toughen. Seeking to control each other rather than to serve one another trustfully, we engage in a power struggle. As Victor Hamilton wrote, "The two who once reigned as one now attempt to rule each other."[4]

Consider the man. Cut off from his heart, compulsive and troubled by work-related concerns, he may use his power harshly toward the woman. Traditionally this expresses itself in a misuse of his authority. Barth described the tyrant who uses his masculine power as an "instrument for seizing and exerting power in favor of his supposed masculine dignity and honor."[5] This tyrant appears to have the right on his side. After all, did not God grant him authority over the woman? Yet his rule is not motivated by a selfless desire to protect her and preserve her honor. Rather, his power is self-serving and originates in a futile effort to bolster his own flagging sense of self.

Some women do not question such mistreatment but rather meekly submit to it. Usually this is because they believe that women are inferior to men and therefore that they deserve the cruelty they are receiving.

Other women arise out of such deadening compliance with a few resurrection tricks of their own. Assuming a false and coy submission designed to control men quietly, they achieve their ends covertly. Manipulation, seduction and passive acts of aggression may be parts of their repertoire. Barth wrote: "The falsely compliant woman complements him [the traditionally broken male] by using a kind of submission that at core is devised to exercise control over him; in her refusal to accept his false expression of authority, she sins by now grasping to control him."[6]

Then again, a woman may arise out of her injured state determined to not be subject to a man at all. Nothing covert here—she is determined to assume leadership in the relationship. This leadership will enable her to live in freedom from the man. He becomes less; she, more. Barth wrote of this response too:

> As the offended and humiliated party, woman doesn't have right on her side, but she has the appearance of right. And in this appearance of right, conjoined with the demonic power of her very weakness, she can in fact become the stronger and man the weaker. . . . The weak man will become continually weaker through the rebellion of his wife, and the rebellious wife continually more rebellious through the weakness of her husband. In short, the order will be continually loosened and disrupted.[7]

A weak man is one who learns early on how to submit to, and comply with, an angry and controlling woman. This may begin in childhood with his mother and continue throughout his adulthood. Such a man fails to lead in relation to woman. Unlike the tyrannous man who engenders fear in a woman through his abuses of power, the weak man lives without power. He abdicates his call to act as an initiator and protector in relation to a woman in his life. He may fear her displeasure and will act only to placate her. This is especially true in cases where the man has injured the woman. The strength of her anger and pain prevails, with his hands tied by his shame and failure.

After hearing me speak on this subject, an artist in Switzerland brought into the conference one of her sculptures. She had fashioned a bold and beautiful bronze of a naked woman. This woman stood regally, her head high and held slightly back upon a torso that gleamed and seemed to radiate confidence. Behind her knelt a clay figure of a man, prostrate. He seemed to be atoning for an unforgivable sin. She, on the other hand, bore a new freedom. Free from him, her independent future appeared boundless. Later on, the artist described the sculpture as a depiction of her parents' loveless marriage, one marred early on by the adultery of the husband.

The sculpture reminds us that power plays between couples can leave a devastating legacy for the offspring of such unions. It reminds us as well that God's order is continually disrupted by the bruising of masculine authority and feminine response. Instead of being united, the two genders, in their fallen state, vie with one another.[8] This comes out frequently in the area of sex.

SEXUAL BROKENNESS

Dehumanized heterosexuality becomes a source of other sins. As parents model cruel and disrespectful relating to their children, a new generation acquires faulty beliefs and attitudes. These children, once grown up, may struggle to honor their commitments as well as to honor themselves and others. The broken image of God in one generation thus can become a source of more extreme expressions of sexual and relational brokenness in the next.

Consider the effect of sexual sin and unfaithfulness. Trust is based on the ability to make and to keep promises to one another. This trust applies pointedly to sexual fidelity. Adam and Eve sealed their commitment to one another with the gift of their bodies. Intercourse made them one. In fact, what set this relationship apart from all others was the sacred offering of their bodies to each other. The advent of sin and the fig leaf signified a new capacity for the couple to withhold themselves from one another, even to use their sexuality to block and counter the other.

Although designed to reveal the powerful good of God's provision for humanity, sexuality can promote and empower the fallen self. This occurs when sexual desire is aroused and expression conceived outside of a lifetime commitment. Split off from the vow to become an increasingly good gift to another, sexual expression violates the nature of the gift itself. It fails to truly enhance her femininity and his masculinity.

"Coitus without co-existence . . . is demonic," declared Karl Barth.[9] He meant that sex without commitment empowers pleasure but weakens humanity's capacity to make and keep the promises that engender trust. This applies not only to the adults involved but also to the children who inherit the legacy of uncommitted sex from their parents.

I remember coaching an especially gifted ten-year-old baseball player. Jon played shortstop better than anyone else on the team. His father assisted me in coaching (I needed all the help I could get!) and was in fact a much better athlete than I was. Jon's father took pride in his son, who was apparently following in his dad's footsteps.

One day the father did not show up, and Jon barely got through the game. He could not carry out even minor plays and cried at his failures. I discovered afterward that Jon's father had left his mother for another woman. Jon muddled through the rest of the season without his father.

Adultery disables lives. In particular, adultery scrambles how one experiences his or her passed-over marriage partner. Outside of the hard realities of domestic life, the new lover appears ideal, the answer to one's emotional and physical needs. In contrast, the existing partner seems like a drudge, inseparable from the realities of everyday life. Consequently, adultery is conceived in illusion and spawns new and cruel illusions about one's "right" to self-fulfillment. These are lies that shatter those left behind.

Adultery fits under the category of fornication, which includes any sexual act performed outside of heterosexual marriage. These actions emerge out of the broken complementarity we have discussed. Fornication is often a flight from the prospect of commitment and genuine self-giving.

Instead of enhancing its participants, fornication reduces one to the object of the other's physical desire. Each partner becomes a collection of body parts, sensual and soulless. Split off from the profound emotion that emerges out of hard-won commitment, sexual excitement results in a "closing down of the horizon of mind and heart."[10]

But its bitter fruit is retained in the mind nevertheless. Multiple sexual partnerships become encoded on the brain. Memory then contains these alien bondings where only one was intended. Through the powerful recall of our memories, we live with false lovers long after the affairs are over.[11]

Uncommitted sex disintegrates the self. It weakens the capacity for mature self-giving. Instead of expressing love and deepening commitment, sex can serve as a futile means of proving one's virility, of securing an illusion of love or merely of pleasuring oneself. In essence, illicit sex is mutual masturbation. One partakes of "it," not the whole of another human being. One need not even remove one's fig leaf.

Fornication conceals who we are as bearers of God's image in our sexuality and gender. It is "a violation of the principle of life. . . . That which was instilled into humankind at creation to continue God's creative work was then used to desecrate the temple in which humankind resided."[12]

Its effect? To weaken our capacity to make and keep our promises to one another. This applies to premarital fornication and of course to the betrayal of vows in extramarital unions. The result is a shattering of the original capacity for communion that God intended for humanity.[13]

And it destabilizes children. A parent's sexual infidelity subjects his or her children to the threat of love's withdrawal as parents expend their energy on the evil at hand—nursing wounds of deception and betrayal, mounting defenses and offenses, moving on to the next family.

Despite these evil effects, fornication remains common practice, just as it has been since gaining new "respectability" in the sexual revolution.

BITTER FRUIT OF THE SEXUAL REVOLUTION

In the 1960s a new generation throughout the Western world heralded the freedom to fornicate. Fueled in part by the hypocrisy of the flat and unconvincing marriages that conceived them, as well as by good old-fashioned rebellion, they cast off restraint and determined to love nakedly, without commitment. What emerged from that era was an elusive, self-centered idealism that erased the boundaries of heterosexual marriage. Marriage vows were deemed either unnecessary or temporary, to be broken when one partner no longer felt fulfilled by the other.

Though commendable in their assessment that heterosexual love could be more than the uninspired formalism of previous generations, these sexual revolutionaries did more harm than good. They devastated the context that could engender love and trust for the next generation. Tragically shortsighted in their take on freedom, they have left us a bitter inheritance.

Consider these facts in regard to divorce. At the turn of the twentieth century, three out of every one thousand marriages ended in divorce. Currently one out of every three marriages ends in divorce.[14]

The growing number of divorces has prompted numerous studies on the effect of divorce upon children. The results? Overall, the children of divorce have been assessed as less secure and stable, experiencing a higher degree of rejection, loneliness, anxiety and fear of abandonment than those in intact families. Perhaps most significant, though, has been the effect of the divorce on the children's relational futures. They hold a less favorable view of marriage, are more likely to have sex and become pregnant outside of marriage, and if married, are two to three times more likely to divorce than those whose parents stayed married.[15]

The sexual revolution was significantly empowered by the legalization of abortion in America in 1973. Though we have no statistics on the number of illegal abortions performed before that time, we can safely assume that its legality after 1973 caused the number of abor-

44

tions to skyrocket. This dovetailed with the increasing number of unwanted pregnancies incurred because of the sexual revolution. The revolutionaries championed their sexual rights as adults over the right to life of unborn children. Over 34 million abortions occurred between 1973 and 1996. It is estimated today that over 43 percent of all women in America will have an abortion.[16]

Another factor encouraging the sexual revolution was the rise of feminism. First let's give credit where credit is due. Feminist voices have often accurately assessed the cruelty with which men have treated women. They have also insisted that these injustices be rectified. But while feminism has helped identify some of the divides between men and women, it has also created new ones.

Feminism may have freed women personally, but has it freed them to come alongside of men, embracing their feminine power as it is best expressed in harmony with masculine strength? I think not. Some strains of feminism have masculinized women, enabling and encouraging them to live separately from men. In that way feminism has contributed to a self-centered approach to life and relationships.

Broken and confusing expressions of heterosexuality result in other aberrations. Think of the effects of the sexual revolution upon the already battered image of God in humanity. Ideas of complementarity and mutual commitment went out the window. People began representing God as male and female even less than they had been doing before the revolution began.

Skyrocketing divorce rates, the freedom to engage in multiple sexual partnerships, a growing distrust between men and women—with conditions like these, is it any wonder that the sexual revolution brought heterosexuality into question as normative for humanity?

EFFECTS OF BROKEN HETEROSEXUALITY

As the heterosexual marriage covenant was challenged as the context for sexual expression, a small band of practicing homosexuals in New York City rioted against the police outside of Stonewall, a gay bar in

Greenwich Village. That June night in 1968 the modern gay rights movement was born. Sexual brokenness had begotten more sexual brokenness.

Though throughout the seventies and eighties homosexual activism was confined mostly to the large coastal cities of America, its influence expanded in the nineties during the Clinton administration. By the new millennium, popular opinion about homosexuality had changed drastically. Not only were the boundaries for sexual behavior in serious question, but indeed now we ask, "Does gender matter in our sexual relationships?"

Before God it does. Karl Barth rightfully understood God's image in humanity as irrevocably male and female. He wrote, "Since humanity . . . is to be understood in its root as the togetherness of male and female, as the root of this inhumanity there follows the ideal of a masculinity free from woman and a femininity free from man. . . . The command of God shows him irrefutably—in clear contradiction to his own theories—that as a man he can only be genuinely human with woman, or as a woman with man."[17]

The emergence of homosexuals as an organized force, insisting on rights comparable to those of heterosexuals, is a clear violation of God's intention for humanity. It issues out of the same source of sin and brokenness that distorts the image of God heterosexually. No wonder that a man bound to broken expressions of heterosexuality—Bill Clinton—was more instrumental than any other American in mobilizing the gay community as a powerful national front.

A recent survey discovered that the number of American women engaging in gay sex multiplied fifteen times between 1988 and 1998 and that the number of American men who engaged homosexually doubled during the same period. Those who conducted the study surmise that positive images of gay people in the media, along with lowered legal and economic barriers, have made it easier for people to act on same-sex desires. But why the huge escalation in homosexual behavior for women? Women in the new millennium possess a new freedom to express themselves both homosexually and heterosexually. They are now free "to consider family structures and sexual partnerships that do not include men," concluded the experts.[18]

A young English woman summarized it well for me when she said, "Of course I slept around a lot with guys. But something else began to happen. Some of my girlfriends started to sleep with each other. I realized the next thing we were heading toward was each other! My friends could now become lovers. That kind of freaked me out."

Psychologist Drew Pinsky supported her perception when he said, "More teenagers and young adults are experimenting with homosexuality and bisexuality. All of a sudden, . . . it just became the topic. . . . It was not just considered OK, . . . it was endorsed, . . . it was cool."[19]

With such trends under way, what will the new millennium hold? Perhaps a disregard for maleness or femaleness altogether. In his high view of God's image, particularly the relation of man to woman and woman to man, Barth asserted that rejection of one's gender "is the starting point of flight from God."[20] To reject one's gender is to defy the Creator and his call for all people to act humanly toward the opposite gender.

A recent article in the *Los Angeles Times* heralded the coming of age of the transgender movement, made up of those seeking to change genders. According to the article's author, "Buoyed by the success of the gay and lesbian liberation movement, . . . the transgender community has emerged . . . as a new voice in social activism." Its aim is to push the limits of gender identification. "Although gender is an identity we are born with, . . . it is too great and varied a force to shoehorn into those ubiquitous boxes marked F[emale] and M[ale]."[21] Commenting on the movement, a sociologist stated, "This is the last phase of the sexual identity movement. . . . It will blur gender lines even further."[22]

God's image lies in disrepair. Since their ousting from the garden, Adam and Eve left a trail of sin and brokenness in their relationship that humanity has followed blindly for centuries. We still bear the divine image. God in his faithfulness still upholds us as male and female, capable of becoming good gifts for each other. But the brokenness of that image is our inheritance as well.

Gratefully, God can restore us. He can resurrect what is true in us out of the mire of our relational and sexual brokenness. That restoration occurs one layer at a time, one man and woman at a time, through the cross of Jesus Christ. He longs to unveil the beauty of his original design in us and empower those weakened by sin and brokenness to love well.

3

STRENGTH TO LOVE WELL

Mike and Katie had been at war for months. They knew their marriage needed help, but they did not know where or how to get that help. Someone told them about the group that was meeting at their church for people with relational dysfunctions. They went and that night they expressed publicly for the first time the source of their conflict.

About one year before, Mike had confessed to his wife a longstanding addiction to Internet pornography. For the first time, he felt a weight of guilt and shame lifting. His wife, who had known nothing about his sin, did not experience release. Instead she felt weighed down by fear and betrayal. Her husband's confession had rendered her powerless. Meanwhile Mike could not understand why his wife could not move on with him to greater freedom. He resented her anger and suspicion; she resented his selfish concerns and inability to comprehend how wounded she was.

A wise caregiver in the group pointed out the problem. "Mike, your confession was the beginning of resurrection. The death of sin began to lift off you. But for you, Katie, that was the beginning of a crucifixion—dying to who you thought Mike was." A light dawned for both. Each could see that the other had to carry the cross in the crisis, but in different ways.

That night they renewed their commitment to taking hold of Jesus' way for the repair of their marriage. Centered on him, and surrounded by loving fellow believers, they began the process of healing that would replace the hostility that had marked their marriage. They began to lay down their swords and cleave to the cross. Their marriage has endured, only now with greater purity, honesty and empathy toward one another.

Jesus is the master reconciler. When he was raised up at Calvary, he bore the weight of our sin and its wounding effects. Through his broken body and shed blood, he erased the gender divide. And in his resurrection Jesus enables men and women to once again become good gifts to one another. He invites us to lay down our swords toward one another. He in turn grants us his cross as the source and sustaining power of our freedom to love others.

THE CROSS FOR THE SWORD

Paul wrote the following about the cross in regard to the divide between Jew and Greek. I apply it to the divide between men and women. "[Christ] himself is our peace, who has made the two one and has destroyed the barrier, the dividing wall of hostility. . . . His purpose was to create in himself one new man out of the two, thus making peace, and in this one body to reconcile both of them to God through the cross, by which he put to death their hostility" (Eph 2:14-16).

How apparent is this hostility! Within our world, and within ourselves, we behold the breakdown of trust between men and women. It is far more pervasive than any exotic perversion. Cycles of cruelty and disrespect that result in broken commitments are spinning out of control today, leaving men and women disoriented and damaged. Out of the wreckage, children emerge into a relational sphere shadowed by the failure of the adults in their lives to keep their promises of love. Is it any wonder that rates of divorce and unwed partnerships are at an all-time high?

From this bitter fruit emerge strains of gender and sexual distortion: sexual addictions, abuse, homosexuality, fetishes, pedophilia, transvestitism and transsexualism. Though we can never wholly grasp the complex interplay of factors that influence such distortions, let one thing be clear: homosexuality and other forms of brokenness are symptoms of a greater breakdown between men and women. It is the traditional hostility between men and women that powerfully influences such variations.

Most of us can perceive in ourselves a window to this greater war, not necessarily in extreme expressions of brokenness, but in the temptation toward hostility with others. We each bear memories of wounding and mistrust in relation to the opposite gender. The other's very difference from us becomes a point of suspicion. We fear that his greater strength or her greater wisdom will be used against us. We then block and counter the other, whether it be on the job, at church or at home. Though we love Jesus, we may have to admit that the sword, not his cross, marks our view of the opposite gender.

Let us not lose sight of the spiritual warfare involved here. Although the cross of Christ smashed the serpent's head, evil still has power to harass us (Gen 3:15). Our enemy will seek to strike our heel—an image that connotes a limited authority to hinder our efforts at loving others aright. I believe the enemy is particularly invested in disrupting our key relationships. He interferes with our efforts to love.

And yet we must persist, especially in our marriages.

MAKING OUR MARRIAGES WORK

Recent statistics suggest that the divorce rate among evangelical Christians is slightly greater than the national average.[1] That represents the power of the sword, not of the cross. But consider what we do when we marry: we invoke God's presence as we commit ourselves to one another. He enters into the union with us. Then we must learn to appropriate the power of the cross in our marriages. That includes taking authority over the one who strikes our heel as we choose to persist in love.

I remember a particularly intense argument between Annette and me. In the midst of that argument I had such contempt for her—the way she needed me, her different perspective on an issue, the power of her tongue and emotions as we sought resolution. Her very difference as a woman provoked and appeared to undercut me.

Though we had pretty good disciplines of communication and prayer together, the conflict had so escalated that reasonable discourse seemed impossible. Forget about humble agreement in prayer! We were both at our wit's end.

I wanted to leave her. And for the first time in our marriage, I did. I packed a few things and left the scene of the domestic crime. On my way out I announced that I was leaving the marriage.

A few miles later I realized that my wife and I were under profound spiritual warfare. The enemy of our souls was not only nipping at our heels; he was goading us into dissolving our vows!

I pleaded the power of the cross over the whole mess. I did not know how to resolve the argument, but I had the presence of mind to cleave to the Lord, to humble myself as he did and to place my hopelessness and my inability to love in his hands. Jesus, who bore all division and hostility between men and women on the cross, bore my contribution.

The Lord then urged me to humble myself to Annette, to confess my part in the mess. I thought, *No way! With her sharp tongue, she will slice me in two!* Thankfully, however, I returned and humbled myself for my sin. That freed Annette to do the same. We still had a big issue to work out, but as we both turned to Jesus, he crushed the enemy's schemes. He called us onto the level playing field of his death and new life where we could work out the problem.

Annette and I are both very verbal and very strong-willed. Our four children know when Mom and Dad are having a disagreement. We do not stew or simmer; we tend to boil quickly, often resulting in charged and even amusing interchanges marked by frustration and an occasional sob. To the kids, it is not the sweetest expression of marital harmony. But neither does it terrorize them. They are certain that

Mom and Dad will work it out. They witness our resolution in minutes, not hours or days. They hear words of forgiveness. They know that the cross is operative in the lives of the most influential man and woman in their lives.

LEAVING A LEGACY FOR OUR CHILDREN

The cross beckons to us to lay down our swords. Doing so frees us to leave a legacy of love to those impacted most by our relationships. God made that clear to me during a recent meeting of people who had experienced brokenness.

I looked around the room and saw a variety of saints marred by sin and wounding in their relationships. God's image in them appeared as beautiful as it was broken. Crushed by addiction and abuse, tempted by the pleasures of the world and disillusioned by broken relationships, the group gathered around the cross, focusing on Christ's suffering that gave rise to life and holy power. I noticed that night how each participant was becoming lighter, more free to love others honestly.

At church the following Sunday I saw one of the group's participants walking with her husband and children. With the group's help, she had successfully warded off the desire to have an affair in light of a stagnant marriage, then had found tools to enhance her marriage. I watched her and thought of the legacy of committed love she would pass down to her kids. Instead of the sword of hostility and secrecy that adultery forges, she would manifest the power of the cross to them.

I want to highlight three dimensions of the authority of the cross to replace our hostility toward one another. These three are (1) the simplicity of the cross in light of our human complexity, (2) the blessing of crises and (3) the power of hope amid the hard realities we face in our relationships. All three are mediated by the community of the cross. We cannot talk authoritatively about the healing power of the cross without our fellow believers—the broken body of Christ whose very weakness can become the ground for holy, healing power.

John Stott wrote, "The very purpose of [Christ's] self-giving on the cross was not just to save isolated individuals, and so perpetuate their loneliness, but to create a new community whose members would belong to him, and love one another. . . . The community of Christ would be nothing less than a renewed and reunited humanity, of which he as the second Adam would be head."[2]

In that community we discover the simplicity of the cross.

SIMPLICITY OF THE CROSS

We are admittedly complex in our brokenness. Patterns of thought and feeling in oneself or in another can defy our understanding. But God knows. And the cross testifies to the sure rhythm of healing, our surrendering to the new life Christ offers. He grants us a choice: will we clench our fist or open our hand to him?

This is particularly relevant to the hostility we may feel toward another, especially someone of the opposite gender. We can readily get stuck on his or her brokenness. Feeling powerless because of the more obvious darkness in the other's life, we may retreat into a defensive posture. Our lives become overshadowed by what the other is or is not doing. So Jesus in his mercy grants us an invitation to come as we are to him, taking full responsibility for the hostility in our hearts. This is the beginning of freedom.

A Christian claim to healing or release in relationships can never bypass the cross. In his excellent book *The Crucified God* Jürgen Moltmann calls us to embrace "the cross [as] the test of everything which deserves to be called Christian."[3] For him, the immovable center of Christianity is the "resurrection of the crucified Christ, and the cross of the risen Christ."[4]

That simple, profound center, with its rhythm of crucifixion followed by resurrection, is our key to healing. Will we allow Jesus to bear sin in all of its dimensions in our lives—our shame, our wounds, our wrongdoing—so that he can empower us to love well, especially where we are weak?

Moltmann wrote, "To know God in the cross of Christ is a crucifying form of knowledge, because it shatters everything to which a man can hold and on which he can build, both his works and his knowledge of reality, and precisely in so doing sets him free."[5] Paul, a brilliant thinker, grasped the freedom of such simplicity. And he knew the bondage of complicating the message. Thus, to the vulnerable Corinthians, Paul proclaimed the real message and messenger—Christ crucified in weakness, yet alive by God's power, and Paul himself, weak and yet empowered by Christ.

CRISES AND THE CROSS

Our capacity to grasp the relevance of the cross may hinge upon relational crises. Sometimes we need to be woken up by disastrous events that provoke our surrender to Christ. Without harsh realities before us, we might remain in blissful darkness. We can choose not to see what is.

Hans Weber said that the cross "always represents the challenge of a definite situation, where the crucified Christ leads to a crisis of certain human aspirations and where he is at the same time proclaimed as the essence of a new existence."[6] To put it another way, our relational aspirations may involve certain controlling mechanisms we employ to keep truth at bay. When they fall apart, we may be ready for surrender to Christ and the hope of new life.

I see this often with long-standing Christians. They love Jesus and are faithful to him as best they can be, but when their personal worlds start to crumble, they expend Herculean efforts to keep the walls from collapsing.

This is where we as the community of the cross must be patient and yet truthful. We do a great disservice to others by complying with the deception of denial. At the same time, we must prayerfully seek the timing and the words that best help the parties involved face the truth of their lives.

Annette and I worked with a couple for several years. The husband's addictions began to manifest themselves during the strain of work pressures. His spouse was a battered wife but a survivor. It took many months for her to stop denying the impact of the grave distress both of them were in. Though she was more obviously the victim, she was one with her husband in seeking to maintain the myth of order.

Finally she made the crisis public by separating from her husband for an extended season. Annette and I stood with her as she made one of the hardest decisions of her life. That crisis woke up her husband. And the community around them. No longer was the brokenness of the marriage a secret.

In that season both spouses faced the cross, dying to their delusions. But they also enjoyed the slow resurrection of truth and grace in their lives, first individually and then as a couple. Today the two share a relationship that is free from addiction and abuse. They have nothing to hide and much to be grateful for.

God is merciful to bear with us when our weaknesses seep out of containment and into sin. Sometimes we are aware of our need to be saved only when we face what is destroying us. Then we have to choose: Jesus or the slow strangulation of sin. Finally we may be ready to give our lives away to the One who can strengthen us with divine love.

THE CROSS AND HOPE

As the community of the cross surrounds those in crisis, we help them to behold the hope of resurrection that shines upon their hard circumstance. Amid the relational wreckage, Jesus is present, willing to assume sin in all its diverse expressions.

The prophet Isaiah spoke of the Suffering Servant who would bear the weight of our infirmities and sorrows (Is 53:4). These words are well translated from the Hebrew as "the sickness of sin."[7] That includes the reverberating effects of disobedience—sin and wounds, the inexplicable losses we endure this side of heaven, the disorder wrought by affliction of many kinds. Jesus in his powerful simplicity grants us hope amid the temptation to despair as we face the realities of our lives.

This hope is crucial as we seek to walk out of sexual and relational brokenness. We have an advocate in the suffering Lord of glory. His fullness—both crucified and resurrected—becomes our hope as never before. Moltmann wrote that hope lies "in the situation of the crucified God, and is recognized by insight into the *pathos* of the loving and suffering God. The central symbol of Christian hope, the resurrection, is expressly related to the assumption of all human reality by God, including that reality which is spoilt by sin and condemned to death. It therefore represents a hope which is indissolubly coupled with the most intensive sense of reality."[8]

The community reminds us of that hope as we gather before the cross. Indeed that is perhaps the main reason why we meet. We encourage one another with the truth that Jesus suffered but now reigns. In the light of his victory we find hope—a hope mediated by those a little further along in their own cross walk.

In our need, if we are seeking healing with the community of Jesus, we discover individuals and couples who have faced the hard truth of their lives. Something woke them up from the sweet drowsiness of denial. God in his mercy invited their surrender. And in the slow resurrection that followed, these men and women learned truths that become lifelines to those of us just beginning the journey.

Their hope, tempered by hard reality, compels us to forsake our swords. We lay down the artillery of sin and denial. We dare to look at the hostility such deception has wrought in our key relationships. The One whose image we bear shines through our fragile humanity. He becomes the hope of our lives, progressively freeing us to represent him in how we love others.

Simply put, the cross possesses the power to reconcile us to our true selves, whole-enough representatives of God's image, male and female. The ministry of reconciliation applies to the dividing wall within ourselves. Until we embrace the good gift of who he has made us to be, we may struggle to love others.

THE CROSS AND THE NEW CREATION

In union with Christ we become new creations. Something has

changed. Jesus has subordinated the power of sin and death at work in our personal identities. He has also laid claim to our highest, truest selves. Paul wrote,

> [Christ] died for all, that those who live should no longer live for themselves but for him who died for them and was raised again. . . . Therefore, if anyone is in Christ, he is a new creation; the old has gone, the new has come! All this is from God, who reconciled us to himself through Christ and gave us the ministry of reconciliation: that God was reconciling the world to himself in Christ, not counting men's sins against them. And he has committed to us the message of reconciliation. (2 Cor 5:15, 17-19)

In other words, Christ reconciles us to himself. Our real selves emerge in that union with him. And out of that posture of yielding to him, we discover a new basis for understanding our adequacy and security as human beings. Jesus reconciles us to who we are as good gifts; we can then exercise the truth of the new creation in our relationships.

I discovered this early on in my Christian walk. My reference point in the beginning was as a homosexual man—what I thought of as my "gay self." God challenged that identity through his Word and his community. Though I had to contend with a network of harmful thoughts and desires, Jesus did not want that network to define me. He wanted to be my reference point.

I began to see clearly. Through the cross Jesus had subordinated the power of the gay self to who I was as a new creation. In union with him I could begin to accept that truth. Its spiritual power began to translate into my relationships.

The community helped out here by not treating me as a special case. I had some unique needs and distortions, but none was too profound for the Lord of the new creation. They understood what was going on and were always on my side, pointing me to the solution in Christ.

Jesus must become our mirror when we ask the question "Who am I?" He alone should possess the power to define our primary identity. Yet even as Christians we still gaze inordinately into the reflection of the world, our feelings and the sum total of our past experiences. C. S. Lewis wrote, "Your real, new self (which is Christ's and also yours, and yours just because it is his) will not come as long as you are looking for it. It will come when you are looking for Him."[9]

Scripture challenged me here. According to Genesis (with a little help from Karl Barth's astute commentary), I discovered that I was not exempt from bearing God's image. He called me to represent him by becoming a good gift to the opposite gender. When the men in my community urged me to consider that calling, I balked. I was tempted to use my old gay self as to why I could not engage seriously with women.

Certainly I needed to grow and mature in many ways. But my background did not determine my relational destiny; Jesus did. And in union with him the new creation in me began to grasp that his work of reconciliation liberated my true heterosexual identity. In time, following a season of in-depth healing, I began to date the woman who eventually became my wife. And in the process I discovered something important about myself and my gender identity.

THE CROSS AND GENDER SECURITY

Underneath my homosexual identity lay a great deal of uncertainty. I did not like the kind of man I was. My masculinity had been the main area of bruising in my childhood and teenage years. My gender identity, in fact, was the part of me to which I was least reconciled. I needed the cross of Christ.

In order to be reconciled to the man God had created me to be, I had to die to old and false words I had received about my masculinity and live to his true word—his yes to who I was as a bearer of the divine image. So I began to meditate upon a Franciscan cross in my living room. That cross is unusual in its depiction of Christ as crucified and yet with his eyes open and his arms outstretched. It conveys power-fully the reality of the risen Christ.

The cross compelled me to lay down my gender insecurities. I sub-mitted to God my lies and fears concerning my gender as well as memories of gender harassment. I also would confess any homosexual yearnings, which to me were another indication of gender insecurity. In turn, God was faithful to empower me with his advocacy. He would anchor me again and again in the truth of who I was as a new creation—a man whole enough in him. After many such cross walks, I began to be free of gender inadequacy.

Jesus' cross is the source. All I had to do was discover that truth through repeated visits to the cross. And even now, when I am tempted to define myself as less than a new creation, the cross brings me back to reality. Jesus empowers me to arise and to love others out of his yes to my manhood.

Most people do not have a background in homosexuality as I do. But the Fall has affected all our identities. In order to become good gifts for others, especially for the opposite gender, we all must go the way of the cross. Truly we must lose our old identities in order to find them afresh in Christ.

THE CROSS AND WHOLE HETEROSEXUALITY

Men and women who go the way of the cross in their personal iden-tities lay the basis for loving the opposite gender uprightly. The reason is simple: God himself, the author and finisher of our humanity, be-comes the stronghold of our lives. Secure in the love and advocacy of God, we dare to give to others and to admit our need for them.

Therein lies our freedom to rightfully yield to the opposite gender. In honoring God as the basis for our identities as male and female, we can seek to become good gifts for others. We thus fulfill Paul's exhor-tation to "submit to one another out of reverence for Christ" (Eph 5:21).

Make no mistake: this posture of surrendering our old identities to

Christ is no small undertaking. Nor is the growing awareness of the new security we discover in him. That transformation occurs over time as we go to the cross both individually and as part of the community.

We all have stubborn attitudes that resist change. But God is gracious. He grants us space and grace to discover the cross as the point of exchange—vestiges of the old identity for the new creation. That, in turn, frees us to become secure as good gifts in our manhood and womanhood.

Without that security in Christ, we struggle to submit to one another, especially to those members of the opposite gender who have wounded us.

FACING OUR HOSTILITY TOWARD THE OTHER

For some of us, the opposite gender has long represented a threat to our well-being. When that is the case, our offering to the other is muted by fear or becomes angry and defensive. We remain hostile, passively or aggressively. The sword, not the cross, marks our posture toward the other.

Yet we must take seriously Paul's words to us. Having been reconciled by the cross to our true selves—that is, the new creation—we must become agents of reconciliation toward others (2 Cor 5:17-20). That is where we must dare to face our fears and our hostilities toward the opposite gender.

Some of us may be tempted by the illusion that we can avoid the conflict. Many broken ones shut down in relation to the opposite gender, spiritualizing their needs and identities in union with Jesus alone. That is understandable, since Jesus is perfect, while people are painfully fallible. Yet God does not grant us the freedom to avoid our need to work out our salvation together as male and female. He calls us to wrestle with our need, and our fear, of the other. This is where we must exit our prayer closets and engage in real-life relating.

Healing groups are a good place to begin to exercise one's new identity as a man or woman in Christ. In fact, this holy exercise can really occur only in community. And if we take the image of God seriously, we must take the gender challenge seriously in our gatherings. That's why at Desert Stream our groups are always men and women together. There men and women have equal access to leadership. Both genders also express the unique ways in which the topics at hand impact them.

Given the boundaries that make the group a safe place for all (as well as a portion of the meeting for same-sex small groups), each member can grow in two crucial ways. Each person discovers his or her unique voice in relation to the others. And each person grows in appreciation for the unique ways that the others views reality.

Of course, one may also find this journey bumpy, even threatening. Old wounds and insecurities may be revisited. New yearnings may arise as well. We exercise our newfound security with shaky voices, yet as we learn to express our hearts to one another, God is faithful to teach us the fullness of his image—male and female together.

I have learned much from the women I have labored alongside at Desert Stream. Through these female saints I have discovered more of who I am as a man, as well as what I am not, thus underscoring the need for women in the ministry if it is to convey God's fullness. For example, Ann Armstrong's leadership in our intercessory ministry has enabled us to go places in the Spirit that I believe would have been impossible without her.

Ann receives things profoundly and passionately. Her feminine soul is a deep well. This can be awesome and challenging. At times I have struggled with her interpretation of things, even as she has wrestled with mine. On occasion I have had to set boundaries with her as to what is appropriate in certain settings. I have had to stand in my role as leader, even as she has risked standing in her unique prophetic intercessory call. Our gifts differ, but together we have sought to work them out as honestly and forthrightly as possible—she as a woman, I as a man.

HOLY STRUGGLE

In every cross-centered heterosexual relationship, we struggle. We can agree with Barth when he said, "Man is unsettled by woman and woman by man. . . . Why are you so different from myself? Can and will you guarantee that your mode of life which disconcerts me is also human?"[10] We stand in a certain creative tension. The cross protects that good tension; it wards off hostility by inviting us into the fullness of the divine image, which is ours only through embracing the other.

There, at the cross, we seek to behold Jesus between us. He mediates his way through us. The cross reminds us that this other was created in God's image, not our own. Thus his or her offering is a gift that should be received freely, as from God. We must be wary of interpreting it through our own gender grid. Our way is not the only way.

We discover that our gender voice is not enough on its own. That is why a community made up of people all from the same gender cannot wholly represent God. The clarity and well-being of one's maleness or femaleness depends on openness to, and reliance upon, one's gender counterpart.

We naturally want to conform the other to our own way of seeing. Instead, though, we must create space for the other's vantage point. We learn the discipline of listening to how the other perceives reality. Unless we do this, we fracture God's intention for his image.

This is a discipline. Discovering the value of our own voices must be matched by welcoming the voice of the other. Something wonderful happens here: in seeking to bless and be blessed in one's gender vantage point, the distinction between male and female becomes increasingly clear. A man is freer to be masculine; a woman is freer to be an essentially feminine creation.

In reflecting upon that challenge artistically, the artist Van Gogh mused, "One learns so much from the constant comparing of the masculine figure with the feminine, which are always and in everything so totally different. It may be 'supremely' difficult, but what would art and what would life be without it?"[11]

Difficult, yes. Although cross-centered heterosexuality frees us to embrace the other's difference while better understanding and accepting our own, it can also vex and frustrate us. At times we are tempted to retreat into our same-sex corners. That's because segregating is easier, especially when one's history is marked by hostility toward the other.

This was true of Sonja Stark, whom I shared about in chapter one. Her experience of men had been pretty rotten, both inside and outside the church. She was thus vulnerable to transferring a lot of her pain onto me, and I was subject to treating her reactions impatiently. We had more than a few hostile moments on the way to building trust.

The cross prevailed. I learned how to surrender to Jesus when I was tempted to lash out at her. As she realized that I could hear her respectfully, even if I did not always agree with her, she softened. We replaced the sword with the cross. As a result, we together have advanced the gospel far more effectively than would have been the case had we gone separate ways.

RESURRECTION OF THE IMAGE

Often the inspired rhythm of masculine initiative and feminine response is lacking as broken men and women gather before the cross for the first time. The hostility between the sexes has wearied them. Beaten-down men are passive; beaten-down women are defensive and self-contained. But men who discover their identities in Jesus Christ begin to exhibit a holy initiative toward women. And women who are straightening up in Christ, while being softened by him, are free to receive man's blessing.

This occurred in my relationship with Annette early on, before our marriage. I took her by surprise one afternoon at her apartment. The door was slightly open, though no one answered it. When I entered the back room, Annette was in the throes of a painful time—she looked distant and deeply depressed. This was not the lovely, vivacious woman I had dated a few times!

A part of me wanted to back away. I wanted beauty and joy, not her suffering. I did not want to be engulfed by such need. The Spirit prevailed, though, and I continued to reach to her, caring for her in her brokenness.

God challenged me that day. He set a precedent for me to love Annette beyond my comfort zone. In the process I began to grow out of my narcissism. I developed truly masculine "muscle" in my embrace of her. And she responded. In time she began to entrust me with more of her needs, especially painful ones related to her childhood sexual abuse.

It has been truly amazing to experience God's strength at work in the weaknesses that Annette and I brought into the marriage. My gender inadequacy was the "heel" that the enemy targeted in my case, and Annette bore her own bruising that tempted her toward self-reliance. But the community of the cross sufficed. As we have continued to make Jesus our focus—in our personal lives and in our life together— he has established that rhythm of initiative and response in our marriage.

I love the witness of this love in Peter's first letter. He described in 1 Peter 3:1-7 the posture of submissive womanhood. Peter exhorted women to reveal Jesus to the man in "the purity and reverence" of her devotion to Christ (v. 2). This is a posture derived from Christ, not the man. Jesus shines through her—holy strength in her weakness. What could be a slavish or defensive posture becomes for the upright woman a gift of inspired beauty. Rather than conceive her tendency to "bend" toward the man, she turns to Christ instead. As a result, she can respond to the man with holy, powerful love. Through Christ she gifts him with the beauty of holiness.

Then Peter implored men to act respectfully toward women, loving them in a way that considers their weakness. In a fallen world the woman is subject to the man in a particular way. The greater power afforded man in an unjust world, coupled with her tendency to "bend" toward that power, renders her uniquely vulnerable.

Peter thus implored man in Christ to consider woman's heightened need for his consideration and respect. Upright in Christ, men are free to give such love. As we crucify our own self-striving and concern at the foot of the cross, we can arise with an inspired sight and power with which to love women. Repentance sensitizes us; we behold women's power and fragile beauty and seek to love them accordingly. Together we unite, power in weakness, co-heirs of "the gracious gift of life" (1 Pet 3:7).

This pattern of initiative and response grants us a powerful glimpse of gender wholeness. Man needs to express his power in blessing woman; woman needs to believe in the truth and integrity of that blessing. In responding to it, she can rise up and bless him as well.

This rhythm between man and woman is not overcome when women and men assume positions of leadership. In truth, how the genders differ and complement each other will become more evident as each responds to God's call.[12] A man occupying a leadership position needs to incorporate the good of the feminine voice in his sphere of authority. He needs greater heart and relational sensitivity. And as a woman exercises her leadership, she needs the special initiative of men's empowering and protection. We still live in a world in which women are suspect in places of power. To retain the good of her true womanhood, not trying to act like a man, a woman will need the support of men as she seeks to lead as a Christ-centered woman.

EXPECTANCY AND LAUGHTER

We forsake our fears and we gather together, male and female. We discover that we are better off as a result of the other. Without the other, we would not be able to grasp the fullness God intends for our humanity. We would not have to face the real hostility we feel, the frustration we experience nor the incredible joy and creativity of living out God's will for his image bearers. Jesus frees us to lay down our swords. We can in turn pick up his cross. Crucifixion unto resurrection. Harmony amid the threat of hostility. Strength in weakness.

And laughter as we wait for the power to come amid our complementary weaknesses.

I recall one incident in which my striving and Annette's insecurity reached a fever pitch. We were doing a conference together on the East Coast and had to fly home on a tight schedule. Annette was particularly anxious. She does not like to travel, especially when the kids are left at home with sitters. Welcome to our airport nightmare.

Our small commuter plane to the big airport was late, enough so that when we taxied to the terminal, I could see our plane to L.A. doing its final preparations for take-off. We raced off the one plane, and I grabbed Annette's hand and propelled her toward the next plane. I was filled with adrenaline and fit from my training as a runner. I had enough strength for two.

Annette resented my dragging her. Less inclined to run, she bruised her heel badly and was wincing by the time we reached the gate. Which had just closed. The flight went without us. Annette was in physical pain, but more than that, she feared for our kids, whose sitter had to leave that night. She was not a happy camper.

I went into action. Annette sat while I raced around the airport—a vain effort as the airport was closing. She had requested some food, but in my running I failed to get any, and now it was too late. Every time I passed her, she looked more and more downcast. And angry at me. Her foul mood drove me into finding a solution. There was none to be found. The airport lost our luggage, rescheduled us on a flight the next day and sent us to a hotel quite a long way from the airport. Many like us were stranded, so that we waited at least an hour for everything that followed: the taxi to the hotel, check-in, a meal at the hotel.

We normally bounce back in such situations. No bounce here. Annette was sullen and speechless. Even my arranging care for our kids through the extra time did not satisfy her. *What more can I do?* I thought.

We finally got to our room at about midnight, five hours after we had landed at the airport and five hours before we had to be back at the same airport. Neither of us wanted to be together. My adrenaline was used up. I had not wanted to talk to her earlier; now, even if I had wanted to, I was too tired. Annette's frown had tightened into a scowl. We sat together in silence, not knowing how to connect.

Then the fire alarm rang out. We staggered out into the hallway with the rest of the bedraggled bunch, where we stood for another fifteen minutes. We all looked so pathetic I had to laugh.

That broke something in me. When we returned to the room, I managed to open up the conversation. At first we got nowhere. I asked Annette if we could pray and simply ask for Jesus to meet us and help us at this impasse. She agreed. His presence afforded both of us peace.

We both laid down our frustrations and fears, especially Annette's concerning the kids. Then she looked at me and said, "Andy, I didn't want you to fix things. I just wanted you to be with me." With that she burst into tears and I held her. She did not want or need my maniacal attempts at getting us home. She just wanted the security of my presence. What a woman!

Through the cross God frees us to lay down our swords. When we do, extending empty hands to him, he empowers us to love each other. Even and especially in our weaknesses.

In the following chapters we will explore in depth the shame, sins and wounds that surround our weaknesses. We do so in order to apply the power of the cross to these areas. All with the goal to welcome Christ's powerful love into our weaknesses.

4

STRENGTH TO LEAVE SHAME BEHIND

Shame is the raincoat of the soul, repelling the living water that would otherwise establish us as the beloved of God. It prevents us from receiving grace and truth where we need them the most. Many factors contribute to shame, but ultimately the problem is that we resist the reality of the Father's love. We believe, falsely, that our sin and weakness disqualify us for receiving his love.

But our Father is faithful. Through the cross Jesus removes every attitude that repels the truth of the Father's love for us. That love surpasses the cursed thought patterns collected over a lifetime of pain.

Though thick and well suited to repel love, our "shame coats" are no match for God's love for us, a love revealed at Calvary.

GOOD VERSUS BAD SHAME

Shame defies simple definition. Its meanings vary. At the very least we can distinguish between two experiences of shame.

The first is appropriate shame. I will refer to this kind as "good shame." Good shame alerts us to our separation from God and others, potentially causing us to cry out to God for mercy. And when we do so, God replaces our fig leaves with robes of righteousness—garments that lend form and order to our relationships.

I will never forget the shame I felt one night in flight from God. I sought out a lover who at the last minute called off the engagement.

I felt exposed and naked, acutely aware of my separation from God and his purposes. I was tempted to hide in my shame. But instead I called out to God and a Christian friend. This holy connection facilitated an exchange of shame for real love. As a result, I desired all the more to deepen communion with real sources of love, rather than to further defile myself.

Good shame can lead us to life. Bad shame, on the other hand, forms a "shame coat," causing us to conclude that we are unworthy of love and honor. The emotion of inferiority, bad shame expresses itself as "an inner torment, a sickness of the soul" that divides us from self, others and God.[1] Bad shame invites the soul to turn on itself rather than to welcome mercy. Bad shame bars us from life.

For some, the roots of bad shame go deep. They reach back to early abuse and abandonment, to long-standing tendencies like addiction and homosexuality, even back to centuries-old expressions of cultural and ethnic shame. For such people, bad shame rests like a thick smog upon their souls, obscuring the light of healing that Christ shines upon them.

Perhaps the distinction between chronic and acute shame may be helpful here. Everyone experiences acute shame once in a while. These are painful moments of exposure, sharp but temporary. Their long-term impact is usually minimal since they are so infrequent. Chronic shame, on the other hand, is a permanent trait based upon repeated shaming experiences. The chronically shamed live diminished lives with little expectation of empowerment and joy. One writer defines them as outcasts from life's feasts.[2]

I remember a man I had the privilege of ministering to for a number of years. His shame was quietly chronic, obvious only when the dark stream of self-hatred surfaced at unexpected moments. We prayed together about many things. I would notice, however, that when we drew nearer to the core issues of sexual struggle and gender inferiority he faced, he would look at me fearfully and searchingly, trying not to cry. Finally I asked him what was going on. "I'm afraid that you will hate me," he said. What was happening was clear: as the sources of his own self-hatred surfaced, he expected me to mirror his chronic shame back to him.

Let's look a bit at the origins of shame.

SHAME AND FALLENNESS

Prior to sin, Adam and Eve experienced a nakedness without shame (Gen 2:25). What is nakedness without shame? Before God, it might mean full disclosure of oneself, unfettered intimacy with the Father. Before one's fellow humanity, nakedness without shame affirms what it means to be male and female as well as the freedom to be a gift to one's gender opposites.[3] Karl Barth described that shameless nakedness between man and woman as occurring when each "recognises the other's distinctive nature" as well as their interdependence.[4]

Upright before the Father, Adam and Eve gave themselves to each other, thus creating the original unity of God's image, male and female. But the entry of sin profoundly disrupted this state of nakedness without shame. "A fundamental disquiet" fell upon humanity.[5] Shame resulted in the first couple from the conscious awareness of their nakedness before God and one another. In this way shameful nakedness conveyed a fracturing of humanity's original unity with God and with each other. Pattison described shame as the "condition of being no longer united with God. It is a mark of separation, differentiation and disunity that is inevitably experienced by all human beings."[6]

Shame as a mark of separation corresponds with fear and flight. Adam in his nakedness hid from God (Gen 3:10).

Shame is also synonymous with the idea of covering or concealment, as the fig leaf suggests.[7] This tendency toward concealment applies to people's relationship with God and with one another. Recognizing the other's nakedness produces conflict. Full disclosure of the self is no longer possible. Having complemented one another well in Eden, Adam and Eve braced for mutual brokenness outside the garden.

The awareness of shame is a reckoning with lost innocence, the realization that one now has the potential to hurt another and to be hurt, to honor God and to dishonor him. Shame is the pervasive effect and affect of sin, not of a particular sin, but of the truth of our separation from the Creator and his high and noble purposes for our humanity, including his intentions for our sexuality and relationships. In his mercy God granted Adam and Eve cover for their shameful nakedness in the form of animal skins (Gen 3:21).

Fallen humanity faces shame—the truth of our separation. Thus, apart from psychological distinctions about shame, we must face the theological reality that everyone bears shame, regardless of ethnicity, culture, family of origin, past experiences and personality. Generally speaking, then, how do we steward the reality of our shame well?

STEWARDING SHAME

The way we handle our shame can make all the difference in what effect it will have in our lives.

For one thing, we should seek to recognize the good in shame. After all, it can be a revelatory, positive emotion.[8] Appropriate shame alerts us to wrongdoing and the need for self-correction. In this way shame "plays a vital role in the development of conscience. . . . The optimal development of conscience depends on adequate and appropriately graded doses of shame."[9] In other words, the emotional experience of separation from what is right and true can be helpful to our moral development. Shame guards self-respect and motivates us to make and maintain boundaries of respect in our relationships. When we cross those boundaries, appropriate shame alerts us emotionally and spiritually to innocence (and respect) lost.[10]

This applies pointedly to relational and sexual intimacy. Shame alerts us to premature uncovering of our humanity to others. The fig leaves of Genesis 3 convey a kind of modesty and privacy related to the yearning of our humanity for union with others. The physical body is now clothed; we are separate from one another in our need for each other, sexual and otherwise. The profound and veiled nature of our sexuality thus corresponds with equal depth to our experience of shame. Paul alluded to this link between sexuality and shame when he referred to sexual sin as unique in its violation of the body (1 Cor 6). Misbegotten sexuality squanders something profound and intimate, thus heightening our shame response. We experience dishonor when we expose our nakedness improperly.

I recall one such exposure as a teenager. I had bought some pornography and I loved it, but at some level I knew it was wrong. I hid the materials, only for them to be discovered by my mother. When she approached me with the materials, my shame level skyrocketed— I was exposed! Yet her response to me resulted in a deepening of self-respect. She did not scorn me but rather pointed out the dehumanizing nature of the material and its ill effect on my humanity. The shame of exposure hurt, but it ultimately bolstered my self-respect. In that encounter seeds of truth and honor were planted that came to fruition years later in my Christian conversion.

A couple of aspects of shame may be helpful here.

First, shame is an appropriate response to the exposure of separation from the Father and his intentions for us. The prophet Jeremiah decried the Israelites who amid idolatry were without shame (Jer 3:3; 6:15; 8:12). The holy nation had intermingled with the spirituality and sexuality of pagan nations. Yet they were brazen in their prostitution, still proud and unblushing in their posture toward God.

Shame is often described as "dishonor, fallen pride" conveyed on the face; in short, a loss of face.[11] Shame registers first on a blushing, downcast face and then pervades the whole of one's being. A person in the throes of shame struggles to sustain eye contact and clear communication.[12] Erik Erikson said, "He who is ashamed would like to force the world not to look at him, not to notice his exposure."[13] The pain of such exposure may distance one from much-needed help. Shame can thus prove resistant to its cure.

Second, guilt possesses a more rational and objective quality than does shame. The latter is more deeply personal; shame floods the whole of the self with acute and dreadful feelings.[14] It can thus immobilize the one who has lost face, rendering him or her passive and hidden. Guilt, on the other hand, is a negative evaluation of a specific behavior. It can be ascribed to specific acts for which one can be forgiven. A guilty person is more likely to act redemptively—to take responsibility for his or her guilt and to do something about it, like seek forgiveness or restitution. A shameful person, saddled by "a global judgment about the whole self as fundamentally bad," may be less inclined to turn toward the light.[15] Exposure means more pain, a descent into self-hatred or rejection, not an ascent into honor and empowerment. Shame deadens the soul in these cases.

What causes the searchlight of love, painful but true and committed to our welfare, to become invasive and abusive? In short, people do. The Father rightfully reveals our separation in order to restore our honor. But in a fallen world we engage with others who dishonor us. Subject to the scrutiny of deceptive eyes and words, we come under the power of bad shame. Wrong shame is the type that we in our sinfulness impose upon others.[16] As we shall see, such shaming can be aimed at various aspects of one's personhood that merge together to become the shame-based self. The latter results from chronic shame—ongoing, persistent experiences of shame.

Here we address the truth that we have been sinned against. Each of us has sinned. But each of us is also subject to the worldly attitudes of others that can accentuate our alienation from God and from each other. These false beliefs, imposed on us by others, can become our own, thus conceiving the affect of inferiority in our souls. This is not a holy poverty of spirit. Instead it is a fortress of lies around the soul.

Let's look now at some of the types of bad shame, beginning with its impact on the Samaritan woman in John 4.

ETHNIC SHAME

The Samaritan woman was no innocent. But much of her shame had nothing to do with sin in her life. She bore the yoke of cultural shame—widely held societal beliefs that bar certain ones from believing they are candidates for God's love.

First she had inherited the shame of her ethnicity. She expressed an awareness of this shame barrier when she questioned Christ as to why a Jew like himself was talking to her, a Samaritan (Jn 4:9). The Samaritans suffered much rejection due to their mixed ancestry, a melding of Gentile and Jewish blood. Their Israelite ancestors had forsaken their spiritual and sexual laws by joining with foreigners. The result? A people who reminded the Samarians of their shame. The Samaritans were scorned, not because of their sin, but due to the shame transferred onto them by their Israelite ancestors.

The Samaritan woman was thus conceived in shame; inferiority was imprinted upon her being. Every unspoken word or averted glance from the superior race—the Jews—would have reminded her of her lesser rank. As Gershen Kaufman says, "People who belong to different cultural and racial groups, and who feel outcast or inferior because of it, live lives of unrelenting exposure to shame. . . . Whenever a group of individuals feels persecuted, disenfranchised, or looked down upon, their resulting shame and powerlessness inevitably become fused."[17]

Imagine the different kind of exposure the Samaritan woman experienced when Jesus conversed with her about living water! His eyes and words—his very presence—began to empower her. Jesus crossed the shame barrier to reach her. He shed light upon her shameful alienation, not to reinforce it but to liberate her from it. That's the kind of liberation many today still need.

One Korean woman caught my attention at a conference. She sat at a different table meal after meal, seeking attentively, with head slightly bowed, to engage with the white majority. She tried for several days, with limited success in connecting herself as part of the whole. I thought, *She has spent her whole life on the outside, looking into a world where she is not wholly known or embraced.* I wept over the shame of difference she and the other non-Anglos face in engaging with us.

Luida Johnson has pioneered the work of our ministry, Desert Stream, among the African American community in Los Angeles. She says the greatest need for healing is not for sexual or even relational brokenness; it is for her people to embrace their ethnicity without shame, to turn from hating themselves because of their skin color. Luida's flock has internalized a culture's belief system, which says in a variety of ways, "White is better." That fortress of lies prevents people of color from receiving favor upon their own ethnic identity.

But while the Samaritan woman would have understood Luida's words about ethnic shame, she also faced other types of cultural shame.

Gender Shame

Another source of shame for the Samaritan woman may have been her gender. Women in her culture were not granted free access to engage with men. That's why Scripture describes the disciples as "surprised to find [Jesus] talking with a woman" (Jn 4:27).

Simply put, the Samaritan's womanhood rendered her less powerful than men in that culture. She assumed a posture of subordination, even inferiority, to them. Such deference is rooted in gender-based shame—the internalized belief that one's gender counts for less than the other gender.

Though much progress has been made in achieving equality be-tween the sexes, we still have a long way to go. The myth of male su-periority still prevails in many circles and is regularly reinforced in some families.

My beloved colleague Helen Bach grew up in a family dominated by a powerful and abusive father. He conveyed to his daughter in no uncertain terms that her worth lay in forsaking any plans for college and career in order to secure and to satisfy a husband. Her mother, beaten down and yet still complying with her husband's inhumane de-mands, bolstered her daughter's gender shame.

Jesus' willingness to look into the Samaritan woman's face and to speak to her respectfully empowered her. He crossed another shame barrier, that of gender inequality, in granting her free access to converse with him. Jesus set an extraordinary precedent for the disciples. Though surprised at Jesus' engaging with her, the disciples remained silent (Jn 4:27). Their leader modeled a new liberty to engage with women, thus pulling down the dividing wall of gender inferiority and shame.

But gender shame is merely cultural; belonging to a certain gender is not an issue of morality. How would Jesus act when the Samaritan woman admitted her sexual misbehavior?

SEXUAL SHAME

Related to gender shame is the inferiority many feel as a result of sexual brokenness. Sins against the body, as Paul calls them (see 1 Cor 6:18), can provoke strong sensations of exposure to, and separation from, others. But appropriate shame related to illicit sex is one thing; believing that one has committed the unforgivable sin is another. Religious cultures are often guilty of magnifying sexual shame to the degree that its stain seems indelible, beyond the grace of God.

In the world of the Samaritan woman, sexual sins ranked among the greatest. We see that attitude in the Pharisee of Luke 7 who was incredulous that Jesus would interact freely with a sinful woman (probably a prostitute). He said to himself, "If this man [Jesus] were a prophet, he would know who is touching him and what kind of woman she is—that she is a sinner" (Lk 7:39). His subtext was clear: holy men do not mingle with the sexually unclean.

Jesus did. He engaged freely and purposefully, though of course not sinfully, with the sexually immoral. To the willing and repentant, he offered living water. In so doing, he revealed a different kingdom than that of the existing religious order. Jesus broke through the inordinate shame his culture imposed upon the sexually broken. In relation to the Samaritan woman, among others described in the Gospels, Jesus revealed the Father's love—a love stronger than the cords of shame that bound sexual sinners.

Not that we should minimize the shame that surrounds sexual brokenness, especially gender brokenness. I refer in particular to those who have had long-standing struggles with homosexual feelings. The Samaritan woman can take us no further here.

Those who struggle with same-sex tendencies face an extraordinary burden of shame. This is due in part to the gender insecurity that often accompanies same-sex feelings. Many who grow up with that vulnerability exhibit signs of difference from their same-sex peer group early on—he is not as tough as the other boys, she is tougher than her more domesticated peers.

Children can be merciless toward their peers who are different, especially those who depart from traditional gender roles. "Youngsters learn at a very early age to avoid doing anything that will earn them the slur 'faggot.' . . . That word is wielded as a weapon to humiliate others."[18] The effect of such humiliation? To imprint on a child a sense of gender inferiority that can contribute to the development of adult homosexuality. Gender shaming becomes a self-fulfilling prophecy—the accusation of "faggot" or "dyke" is realized as one's vulnerability becomes an identity.

I will never forget the gender shaming I experienced in junior high school. Someone had started a rumor—unfounded by any action or proclamation of my own—that I was gay. I became aware of that rumor one day while walking home from school. Before me, on the sidewalk, I read a roughly scrawled message: "Andy Comiskey is a faggot." It stunned me. The next day at school I heard the same accusation throughout the day. The gossip spread like wildfire and burned me for several weeks. The fear of further humiliation intensified to the degree that I eventually went numb inside; I felt like I was floating through a dark night.

While I was walking into a classroom one day, several children began to taunt me loudly and the whole room laughed. Something in me broke. I exited the classroom, then ran into some bushes and hid. I wept and I cried out to God to remove me from the glaring, naked light of exposure. My world had become unsafe. I wanted to leave it.

The shame I already felt in my difference as a male had become unmanageable. Not only was I inferior to the other guys; I was a pervert. I had to be. Others saw something in me that I did not. Two years later I had sex with another guy. A year after that I assumed a gay identity and soon moved into a gay part of town with a male lover.

Gender shame does not cause adult homosexuality, but it contributes to it. I believe that I suffered from a weakened identity as a male and that the taunting weakened me further. But that did not make me gay. Had someone rightfully assessed my need for masculine blessing and affirmation, my choices later on might have been very different.

PROFOUND ROOTS OF SHAME

It is difficult to describe the impact that others' shaming can have on a soul. The depth of shame can seem unfathomable. That one possesses certain weaknesses, personality traits and quirks that set one up for exposure is inevitable. But its inevitability does not dismiss shame's power—it can sear inferiority upon the soul, branding one as bad.

To be sure, certain ones may experience the impact of shame more profoundly than others. For those already sensitive and prone to disempowerment, disqualification becomes a kind of birthright. While others expect and embrace sources of light from without, the chronically shamed brace for exposure. Their garments become thicker to defend the wounded self.

This may be especially true for those whose early experiences of life were less than welcoming. Developmental researchers are unanimous today in assessing the negative impact of a breakdown in parent-child love in one's early childhood. This is especially true of the mother's failure to convey to the child, beginning in infancy, that she or he is wanted. Many things can contribute to this disruption, including the mother's sickness, her preoccupation with other pursuits or anything that prevents her from ensuring the child's care. We feel welcomed in life when we are welcomed.

Conversely, disruptive experiences can imprint a lack of welcome on the child's soul. This is among the most profound sources of separation from love that humanity bears long after childhood. Without adequate parental care, especially attachment to the mother in the first two years, the child can be "entangled in a web of profound uncertainty." If patterns of neglect, humiliation, rejection or abandonment persist, "the child will eventually feel lacking in some essential way, deficient. This is shame."[19]

Chronic shame is synonymous with a pervasive sense of not being wanted. The earlier and more persistent the unwelcoming experiences are, the more toxic the shame. This type of chronic shame engenders a profound sense of ineligibility for love. These "are the seeds of powerlessness, inferiority, weakness, defilement, and unlovability that constitute chronic shame."[20] We see this pattern, for example, in Cam Rimmer's life.

Cam's life began in brokenness, as he was conceived illegitimately. His mother bore the shame of her condition and was rendered nearly destitute. Mentally ill, she abandoned her son, then attempted suicide. A wonderful Christian family adopted Cam and loved him as best they could—a considerable offering. But Cam grew up unable to receive their love. He bore a weight of chronic shame that rendered him unable to love others. As soon as he could, he left home and became a sailor.

While traversing the seas, with alcohol and sex as his best friends, Cam sought to insulate himself from his pain. He married and continued to drink. His condition worsened, as did the marriage. His wife attempted suicide and Cam finally came to grips with his alcohol addiction. Attending Alcoholics Anonymous was the first spiritual step he took, one of many in receiving the Father's love for him. We will look at the restoration of his early wounding later.

SHAME AND CONTEMPT

One thing that resulted from Cam Rimmer's early experiences of chronic shame was self-hatred. Those like Cam who have been subject to profound rejection will often blame themselves. They believe they deserve to be rejected. And like Cam, many seek to assuage the pain of rejection with various addictions. The degradation of addiction produces more shame and self-hatred, and the cycle continues.

The same applies to those who have been humiliated by degrading words and actions. For many, early experiences of abuse translate into an acute sense of being dishonorable. One sees this especially with women who accommodate themselves to degrading relationships with men.

I have worked with many women who tolerate perverse sexual practices and extreme emotional cruelty from the men in their lives. Their reasons for submitting to it? A nearly complete lack of self-respect. Unlike more whole women whose dignity would never permit such treatment, these humiliated ones barely register a complaint. They feel they deserve no better.

Contempt for others can be another result of shame. Here one's shame coat is barbed, ready to puncture anyone who threatens the person with the sort of shaming he or she experienced early in life. The problem is, this coat may ward off both people who present a real threat and those undeserving of such prickly treatment. Depending on the degree of damage done, the contemptuous one may not be able to discern who is actually unsafe. But one thing is sure: the person will come alert like a sentry, ready to defend the threatened child still cowering under the thorny coat.

Another effect of shame is subtler than contempt for self and others. It plays itself out in an extended pattern of role-playing that I call the "good, false self."

THE GOOD, FALSE SELF

When we present an image of ourselves to others that is more capable, more emotionally healthy and more morally upright than we really are, we are projecting a good but false self. Such a projection is misleading and hypocritical, but it is among the most common responses to shame that I have witnessed in my work with men and women coming out of sexual brokenness, especially homosexuality.

Understanding the good, false self as it plays out in people's lives is crucial. In identifying it, we can help men and women to face themselves as they truly are and receive God's mercy in the weaknesses they possess. Without identifying the good, false self, we risk empowering a mere image, behind which the real man or woman remains untouched by the light of Christ. He or she is then capable of great darkness.

The sources of shame empowering the good, false self are twofold. One source is the early experience of shame. The other source is a person's besetting weakness in adulthood, whether that is a same-sex tendency or some other inclination toward brokenness or disorder. These two sources of shame merge and together fuel the formation of the good, false self.

Due to early shaming experiences, and the threat of more to come, the child develops a pattern of compliance. This posture may be characterized as sweet and unassuming. Nothing wrong there, but the formation of such goodness in the false self arises as a defense against the fear that one is flawed and unlovable. The perfect self emerges as an image to guard oneself against the exposure of weakness. The greatest fear of the good, false self is this: "If you really knew me, you wouldn't love me."

In some cases a child receives such a high dosage of shame in his or her life that exposing struggles and failures seems unsafe. To gain acceptance and approval, the good, false self suppresses the reality of its needs and feelings. It averts rejection by changing color, chameleon fashion, according to the shade required in whatever setting the person is in.

The Christian community often approves of the good, false self.

This is especially true of groups that emphasize compliance to human authority. Shamed people often lack a strong sense of their own initiative but may respond readily in submitting to another's. They may also thrive on the favor granted the image of obedience they seek to convey in such settings. This image is the Christian version of the good, false self.

Referring to the kind of people I have just described, Stephen Pattison said, "In their concern for extrinsic recognition and approval, they may also be the kind of people who are 'concerned to show others, self, and God that [they are the] good, kind, caring—even heroic—[people that their] religion celebrates.'"[21] The church often benefits from the obedience of good, false selves. They are useful and unproblematic. Or at least they are some of the time.

For the good, false self is divided. Its other side, the "bad self," is the sum total of all the shame that the person has internalized. It cowers under the threat of exposure. What is safe to expose is the good self. Thus the person feels split and experiences the self as two halves: one good, the other bad. "This splitting of 'good' versus 'bad,' meaning the bad self and the good self, is itself a direct consequence of shame," said Gershen Kaufman.[22]

Splitting keeps a person bound. In that divided place an individual is not free to admit to being a sinner. This signifies a significant gap in a person's moral development. Until one can freely admit one's needs, weaknesses and failures, one cannot experience the grace to be a whole human being. Nor can one honestly reckon with one's flaws.

The danger of the good, false self lies in deception. If one's value seems to be bound up in "goodness," then anything that belies the good-boy or good-girl image must be buried and denied. This is especially true of struggles related to sexuality and particularly homosexuality. The good, false self trembles at references to the topic. (This may partially be due to the condemning and heavy-handed treatment of homosexuality in some Christian circles.) To cope with the anxiety over the exposure of the "bad self," the person may lie to cover up the reality of what is actually going on outside of the sphere (often religious) in which his or her good, false self is celebrated.

A Double Life

The avoidance of the defective self can lead to a double life—the good Christian on one hand, the sexual addict on the other. These "may be tempted to lie to others about things in order to maintain face."[23] Such conflict may actually empower the placating, people-pleasing behaviors of the good, false self. The person strives to maintain a base of security through compliance and conformity. At the same time, the person may be unraveling in his or her sexual and relational sphere.

I have had several experiences with those so profoundly divided that the "bad self" nearly became another person. These were longstanding Christians who had lived a double life for years. Their split enabled them to handle the anxiety of operating in two highly conflictual spheres.

One man was the administrative pastor of a large church. He knew me and the work we were doing and supported it enthusiastically. But the entire time we were relating to each other, he was regularly patronizing houses of prostitution—a behavior over which he felt little or no conflict. Later, though, upon contracting the HIV virus, he confessed to a thirty-year history of sexual addiction. It had begun with pornography use as a teenager while he lived in the home of his father—an angry, remote and demanding pastor of a conservative church.

Another case involved a woman who had a beautiful family and an impressive record of church volunteerism. She entered our Living Waters program on the basis of marital problems. At first she was a model participant—cooperative and helpful at every turn. Then a pattern began to develop. She would attach herself to attractive women in the group, who one at a time would inexplicably drop out of the program. Later on we discovered that outside of the group she was aggressively seeking to seduce these other women. What came to light was an intensive history of shame and abuse from her mother, then a series of intense, short-lived homosexual affairs.

What surprised me most was the dispassionate way she responded to the exposure. Her biggest concern was that others might find out about her behavior, not that her deception was having a devastating effect on those she loved most. Her need for approval was far more profound than her moral and spiritual maturity.

SHAME AND ABUSIVE LEADERSHIP

A young minister-to-be sought our help for a same-sex struggle. Everyone loved this man, and he assumed increasing authority as his ministry experience grew. Hired by a church, he spent much of his energy accommodating others; in turn, he spent less and less time dealing with issues in his own life. Pressures mounted for him as he faced some unexpected domestic crises. He grew more cryptic about his well-being but seemed unflagging in his service.

This man covertly struggled with powerful sexual temptations for teenage boys. Shame over his struggle silenced him. He tried to work off his stress and shame until he befriended a male teenager at church, one vulnerable to his care and affection. This led to him sexually abusing the teenager, then another, until he was exposed and charged.

I cannot tell you the suffering this caused all concerned. It taught me about the awesome power of leadership. When a leader's base is built on the fault line of shame and secrecy, the welfare of others is threatened. Adding to the confusion was the usefulness of this young man's good, false self—the generous compliance from which so many benefited. We can empower the very mechanism in others that distances them from facing the truth of their lives!

The good, false self dies hard. Until it does, shame can drive us not only to serve others but also to blacken the eyes of those we seek to serve. One last story may reinforce the point.

For as long as he can recall, Ben has been the good guy. In his family, as a young Christian and now as a minister, he seeks only to do well; he winces at failure. He is attractive and capable but struggles with a sense of inferiority.

A couple of years ago Ben began to pastor Kim, a beautiful young woman. Ben's wife joined him as he counseled her, although at times he would pray with Kim alone.

Kim, a single parent, began to bond with Ben. Then over time her affection for him grew. Ben loved the attention and secretly gave her cues that he regarded her as special too. Because of Ben's good, false self, he would not admit to anyone the beginnings of this emotional adultery. Such an admission belied his image.

His wife, however, observed what was going on. To save face, Ben played dumb, then joined his wife in feigned outrage at Kim's attraction to him. Ben and his wife confronted her about her feelings. Ashamedly, she admitted them and under the scrutiny of the church leadership left the church.

Ben and his wife felt justified in disciplining this "Jezebel." But in reality Ben had contributed as much as, if not more (given the power of his position) than, Kim to the relationship. His good, false self would just not allow him to admit it. So she alone had to bear the shame of their mutual attraction.

Bad shame tempts us to cover ourselves. We put on shame coats. For some the coat is made up of self-hatred. For others it is woven of contempt toward others. Still others assume a falsely gleaming coat to compensate for the badness within. In these cases shame has disabled one from receiving the love necessary to truly accept himself or herself, weaknesses and all.

Bad shame can be overcome only through the power of a greater love. That love must be stronger than the powerful imprint of human rejection and scorn. The only love that qualifies is the love of Jesus Christ.

THE CROSS AS SHAME'S CURE

On the cross God in Christ endured the ultimate humiliation. For our weaknesses and shame, God allowed himself to become weak and full of shame. God was strung up naked before a mocking, jeering public. He subjected himself to the worst kind of exposure in order to make a way for us, his creation, who have been subject to the exposure of sin and shame ourselves. The Scripture tells us that Christ, "for the joy set before him endured the cross, scorning its shame. . . . Consider him who endured such opposition from sinful men, so that you will not grow weary and lose heart" (Heb 12:2-3).

Let us thus consider further his shaming on the cross. Jesus chose to bear the weight of sin and all of its divisive, shaming effect upon humanity. He did so because he loved us. Sin creates a huge gap between God's highest purposes for us and what we experience as we bungle through life on earth. This separation goes as deep our bones, and we widen the gap in the shameful ways we treat others. Sin thus gives rise to appropriate shame (the realization of sin) and bad shame (sinful attitudes that we impose on others).

Shame is a consequence and a penalty for sin. But God chose to pay that penalty through Jesus Christ's enduring the final act of shaming—his humiliation on the cross. He did so to bear the weight of all sin and shame. In his death he destroyed shame's authority to define us. And in his resurrection he raised up a new humanity who live in the light, radiant and unashamed.

Stephen Pattison wrote, "God has entered into the shame of sin in Jesus[;] human beings now share the objective honour and worthiness that God gives to Jesus. . . . Debilitating shame is transformed so that the only sort of shame that is left is that which pertains to witnessing God's own humility in Christ. This is a shame of proper reverence and respect."[24]

We who have lived as if thousands of eyes look on us as defective and inferior can look to the One, crucified and resurrected, as the single reflection of our value. The cross bears witness of this objective yet life-transforming truth: "God made him who had no sin to be sin for us, so that in him we might become the righteousness of God" (2 Cor 5:21).

The objective witness of the cross is crucial in transforming our shame into honor. As we have seen, shame is intrinsically subjective—personal and acutely felt, tempting one to pronounce global judgments on himself or herself. We thus need a clear and steady witness of the light—the truth that God has acted on our behalf.

The power of Christ's shaming on Calvary has greater authority than the power of personal shame. We must make every effort to cleave to this truth until we internalize it. Indeed, I believe that God intends for the symbolic power of the cross to pervade our reality. In so doing, our awareness of his impartation of honor toward us can displace the shame and dishonor we may still be tempted to ascribe to ourselves.

CLEANSING FROM SHAME

I experience this cross-centered victory as twofold. First, that victory involves the power of resurrection—God's powerful love imparted to us as the basis for our new identities as sons and daughters. But second, putting on the new garments of righteousness also means taking off the old shame coats. Thus the victory over shame must involve the power of God's cleansing.

Through the river of life released at his crucifixion (the blood and water described in John 19:34), Jesus dissolves the shame deposits in us that resist the truth of his love for us. Often when I pray for others or receive prayer myself, I imagine that cleansing stream moving into the deep places of the soul, removing shaming words and pictures while imparting comfort and healing to shame-related wounds. Jesus' healing stream flushes out those sources of inferiority still seeking to define the soul.

Then Christ resurrected extends his righteousness like a coat of honor around us. He lends protection to the fragile soul still emerging out of shame's grip.

I am reminded here of the prodigal son cowering in shame as he returns to his father. The father runs toward his son, then wraps his arms around him and kisses him (Lk 15:20). Affectionately, the father closes the gap between the son's perceived unworthiness and his desire to return to the father (v. 21). He displaces his son's shame with the power of his loving presence. The father then grants his son a robe of honor, the best one possible (v. 22). Having displaced the son's shame with the power of his love, the father clothes him with honor.

Jesus does the same for us, again and again and again. His death on the cross has released a cleansing river that removes shame. And in his resurrection he covers us with a coat of righteousness, fitted and wrapped around us like a holy embrace. His presence is an abiding witness of his desire to exchange our debilitating shame for his honor.

This is an objective work, finalized once and for all at Calvary.

RECEIVING WORDS OF FAVOR

Just as shame can pervade our identity to the degree that it defines us, so does the Father seek to override shame's power by defining us as his beloved sons and daughters. The Scripture is radiantly clear here. Paul wrote:

> When we were children, we were in slavery under the basic principles of the world. But when the time had fully come, God sent his Son, . . . that we might receive the full rights of sons. Because you are sons, God sent the Spirit of his Son into our hearts, the Spirit who calls out, "*Abba,* Father." So you are no longer a slave. (Gal 4:3-7)
>
> You did not receive a spirit that makes you a slave again to fear, but you received the Spirit of sonship. And by him we cry, "*Abba,* Father." The Spirit himself testifies with our spirit that we are God's children. (Rom 8:15-16)

Shame—a basic principle of the fallen world—makes us a slave. Its bondage leads to the fear of exposure and further separation. Only the power of God's greater love can break shame's grip. The Spirit of resurrection anchors us in the new identity and reminds us persistently and profoundly that at our core we belong to the good Father. Through his Spirit in us, he compels us to draw upon him and his acceptance of us as our source, rather than from the toxic wells of shame.

In turn, we can look heavenward as radiant children whose "faces are never covered with shame" (Ps 34:5). Our foundation is sure. We have entered into communion with the Father on the sure basis of Christ crucified and resurrected. Through the cross, God's final shaming, "a precious cornerstone for a sure foundation" (Is 28:16) was laid. From him we derive our freedom as sons and daughters of the Father. Those who enter into relationship with the Father through the Son need "never be put to shame" (Rom 9:33; 10:11).

Nevertheless, our positional freedom as sons and daughters must be worked out in community. The bad shame imposed by fallen humanity must also be surmounted through empowering, nonshaming relationships. Otherwise our hope remains a spiritual abstraction. Bonhoeffer's words ring true: "The Christian in exile sees in the companionship of a fellow Christian a physical sign of the gracious presence of the triune God."[25]

Nonshaming Community

Bad shame exiles us until we meet God in the living witness of men and women who reveal to us the freedom Christ won for us at Calvary. Consider the source of bad shame—the glare of critical, even prejudicial gazes and words from others. In its turn our freedom from shame must be mediated by the new community.

Simply put, we need people who provide new models and new sources of identification for us. The bad effect of social shame can be displaced through relationships that mirror the freedom to be who we are as bearers of God's image. At the same time, others can free us to admit that we are broken by sin and shame and are in need of others.

God's love is perfect and the basis for emerging out of shame. Still, it is the witness of his nonshaming people that frees us to actually grasp at the human level that it is safe to be human—at once a child of God and an imperfect being who dares reveal his fears and flaws to others. Realizing (slowly at first) that we are free to be known in the range of our humanity invites us to remove our shame coats and receive love in their place. This can occur in individual relationships or in group settings.[26]

I have been tremendously blessed by those around me in the worshiping community. My church—the Vineyard Christian Fellowship—has continuously exemplified a nonshaming and affirming attitude toward me as I have struggled with my sexuality. There I exercise the freedom to take off my minister's hat whenever necessary. Through the prayers of others, I can receive at any time the grace of belonging, at once broken and beloved.

Desert Stream Ministries emerged out of such a nonshaming climate. The small groups we offer become part of their sponsor churches. There individuals seeking to arise out of shameful problems discover the nonshaming witness of Jesus in the small-group setting. Now, all over the world, we have a witness of the church freeing individuals to emerge out of shame and into their belovedness. This then frees them to work out real issues of sin and struggle. Let me share with you some of their victories.

I have already mentioned Cam. He received a significant healing of the shame rooted in early abandonment from his mother. Cam had not realized the impact of the breakdown in mother-child bonding until hearing teaching on the subject. During a ministry time for those suffering in that area, Cam began to feel pain in his abdomen—an ache that intensified into an acute wound. Someone prayed for him during this time, gently affirming his connectedness with the Father's all-embracing love for him. In an extraordinary way the Spirit was identifying and breaking the grip of rejection that had been the source of great shame in Cam.

The Spirit administered the truth to Cam of how the Father draws his son to himself, just as a mother bonds with a child. These words from Isaiah rang true to him:

Can a mother forget the baby at her breast
  and have no compassion on the child she has borne?

Though she may forget,
I will not forget you!
See, I have engraved you on the palms of my hands;
your walls are ever before me. (Is 49:15-16)

That day the Father released Cam from the stronghold of abandonment. He did so through insightful teaching, through the power of the Holy Spirit revealing the Father's love and through the gracious mediation of Christ's body. The process of healing continues for Cam. But he is now freer than ever to receive healing intimacy from Jesus and others. He is becoming a radiant receiver of holy love, curing his core shame.

Helen had suffered much abuse from her father and from men in general. She typified the dishonored woman who expects little else. A sense of inferiority hung on her like a cloud. As God and others began to affirm her core value, though, she slowly emerged from her pervasive shame and self-hatred.

She became an assistant leader in Living Waters, a study program offered by Desert Stream Ministries. Stunned and enlivened by the fact that she could be instrumental in helping others, Helen became a group leader. At the same time, she began to set limits with those men in her life who still expected her to receive their dishonor, such as her father. Though challenging for her, these steps indicated her freedom from shame and granted her more freedom. Today she knows and acts upon her intrinsic value as a godly woman.

Earlier I described Ben and the destructive impact of his good, false self with his parishioner Kim. The shame in his life prompted him to develop a self that could only convey its goodness. His role as pastor reinforced the false self, as did the community around him who expected him only to be good. Coming out of the good, false self meant experiencing his shame—namely, the painful truth of his sin and brokenness. This occurred through a pastoral counselor who developed trust with Ben and over time helped him to accept his impoverished self.

Underneath his gleaming coat, Ben was desperately needy for love.

This caring relationship administered a kind of grace to Ben that he had never experienced. His priestly garments had become grave clothes because he had used them to hide himself from the truth of his sin and brokenness. That only reinforced his shame. And the cycle continued—the more shame, the greater the need to be good. Gratefully, Ben received the help he needed to remove the robes and expose himself in a safe and caring relationship. Through it God began to transform how Ben saw himself and God.

Accepting his whole self freed Ben to deal with his sin—the destructive impact of his good, false self. In refusing to admit his own sin, he blamed others. For example, he blamed Kim for their emotional adultery. It took courage for Ben to admit this to his wife and for them together to seek Kim's forgiveness. Ben also faced a greater challenge. He had to choose to surrender the good, false self, this image he had carefully created to hide his shame and brokenness and sin. He had to die to that self.

Powerful love that persists in our lives challenges our false coverings. Like light piercing the haze, love shines on us and invites us to face the truth. That truth involves at once the reality that we are loved and the reality that we are limited, finite human beings whose freedom lies in God's unchanging, unfailing love.

The realization of love will inevitably involve caring individuals who mediate the Father's tenderness to us. We can then begin to face who we really are—broken and precious bearers of God's image.

Christ crucified and resurrected is the objective witness of our freedom from shame. The cross conveys the One who endured scandalous exposure on our behalf. We who bear shame thus have an advocate in Christ. To him we can offer up our experiences of shame again and again. We need not hide. His unveiling at Calvary—his shameful nakedness—frees us to come forth and discover afresh the freedom of exposing our shame to him, receiving in return the garments of compassion and honor that he offers.

5

STRENGTH TO OVERCOME SIN

Bad shame prevents hurting ones from discovering the cross—the only route to freedom from sin. Only when anchored in our status as beloved sons and daughters of God are we free enough to press through the shame and to name what is wrong. As a result of what Jesus has done on the cross, we can proclaim, "God has freed me to acknowledge my sin. Before him, I am free to be a sinner!"

Sin can be erased only through its exposure. And that exposure occurs as one's sin is laid bare through confession before God and other human beings. This is painful. In confession we are exposed once more to the reality of our sin and the appropriate shame and guilt that accompany it. But our exposure is readily eclipsed by the Exposed One. He who bore the weight of all sin and shame bears our own.

This basic tenet of the Christian faith—that God delivers us from sin through confession at the foot of the cross—has been all but lost in our culture today. Even the church seems to be more conversant with her problems, dysfunctions and addictions than she is with confessing her sins. We have forgotten the words that describe our disobedience to God and our disregard for self and others.

The language of sin has been replaced by the secular language of recovery. Without the words of redemption, we struggle to bring a meaningful offering to Christ. How can he bear our burden of sin if we frame it in secular terms? We may receive human empathy, but not the divine absolution that sets our hearts free.

We as a ministry experienced this gap powerfully several years ago. I was in the midst of my seminary education, alive to many new theological and clinical insights. These I shared freely at the first conference Desert Stream sponsored with our dear friend and mentor, Leanne Payne. At the end of our three days together, I asked Leanne for any input she had for us. She replied wisely, "You have wonderful insights. But you are weak in reckoning with the reality of sin in your midst. When you begin to lose the sense of sin, you lose the meaning of the cross. And Christ crucified is the base and source of all healing." Since then, we have made the cross, and confession of sin, central to all we do.

CONFESSION AND COMMUNITY

Confession requires community—the witness of trusted brothers and sisters. I firmly believe that without that witness our efforts to live honestly and wholeheartedly will not work. We as the church must be reminded of the biblical call to gather as sinners in order to be cleansed. John understood "walking in the light" as confession in community. He wrote:

> If we claim to have fellowship with him yet walk in the darkness, we lie and do not live by the truth. But if we walk in the light, as he is in the light, we have fellowship with one another, and the blood of Jesus, his Son, purifies us from all sin.
>
> If we claim to be without sin, we deceive ourselves and the truth is not in us. If we confess our sins, he is faithful and just and will forgive us our sins and purify us from all unrighteousness. (1 Jn 1:6-9)

In this passage John anchored confession in two related truths: our need to acknowledge sin and our need for one another in light of our sin.

Dietrich Bonhoeffer developed this interrelationship further. He drew upon James's exhortation to "confess your sins to each other and pray for each other so that you may be healed" (Jas 5:16). Healing requires confession to one another. In revealing our sin to each other, we detach from deadly sources and unite with the life of Christ present in his body. We are made whole through communion with fellow sinners.

Without confession, we can remain alone, skimming the surface of God's grace in less revealing aspects of fellowship. But in confession comes the "final break-through to fellowship," according to Bonhoeffer.[1] Here we experience a connection with others that rescues us from the domination of sin. That rescue occurs through confession of sin and powerful, repetitive responses of mercy. We are thus enabled to resist what is deadly and to choose life, that is, communion with Jesus through his church.

Many of us have not experienced such freedom in our churches. We may be more familiar with the fellowship of well-heeled saints than with the foot washing of dirty sinners. Bonhoeffer wrote:

> The final break-through to fellowship does not occur, because, though they have fellowship with one another as believers and as devout people, they do not have fellowship as the undevout, as sinners. The pious fellowship permits no one to be a sinner. So everybody must conceal his sin from himself and from the fellowship. We dare not be sinners. Many Christians are unthinkably horrified when a real sinner is suddenly discovered among the righteous. So we remain alone with our sin, living in lies and hypocrisy. The fact is that we *are* sinners.[2]

Jesus is intent on freeing us to be a fellowship of sinners. He will transform his bride through our exposing our rags to each other rather than concealing them behind gleaming shame coats. The scandals of exposed sin among lonely, isolated church leaders have taught us well—we cannot afford to remain alone in our sin. Nor can we afford to entrust our failures (and vulnerabilities toward that end) solely to the "experts," professional confidantes to whom we confess miles away from where we worship. We will discover Jesus in the humble, trustworthy brother or sister next to us. To that one we can confess the deadly offense and thus reenter wholeheartedly into the life of fellowship.

Corporate confession has been the key to my freedom to serve Jesus. I have made known my sin before cardinals and custodians. Not the safe confession of a failure twenty-five years ago, but the struggle for security and sanctity in small, ongoing defeats en route to heaven.

Of this I boast: God grants mercy to the contrite. So I confess boldly my failures before others that they too may seize the grace that comes through confession to others. May my freedom to be a sinner reveal the cross as it is to be found in the community!

God has freed me to be a sinner in his church. He wants to free you as well. It is not easy, but it is the only way to life. In confession to a brother or sister we break through to the cross. We respond to Jesus' invitation to die in order to live.

I have found there are two deaths that confession requires of us. The first is the crucifixion of the social saint.

DYING TO THE FALSE SELF

Through confession we put to death any false image of perfection. With our sin presented in full view of our brother or sister, we cannot hide. We do not even seek refuge in ambiguous descriptions like "struggle," "brokenness" or "weakness." We confess the specific way we have failed. Period. And in such a painful reckoning with what we have done, we die a sinner's death. Bonhoeffer wrote, "In the confession of concrete sins the old man dies a painful, shameful death before the eyes of a brother. Because this humiliation is so hard we continually scheme to evade confessing to a brother."[3]

And scheme we do. While at a conference in another nation, I was working out some conflicts with a beloved colleague there. We were struggling in our working relationship, and I wanted to detach from

97

him and the conference. Nevertheless, at the outset of our conference, we began with our usual time of prayer and confession for the team.

As we waited in quiet, the Spirit convicted me of several sins, including my response to my colleague. I resisted these promptings; I did not want to humble myself. *I will be vulnerable elsewhere,* I concluded. Immediately I knew that if I withheld my offering of confession before the group, the unity and flow of the Spirit would be impeded during the conference. So I admitted my sins without naming the colleague I was having a problem with.

By the end of our time, my colleague and I had the space to work out our differences. My not forsaking confession during the process liberated the grace required to heal the relationship. It was the right thing to do, even if it was humbling.

Public confession actively destroys our pride. It requires the Spirit of the crucified and invites us to follow him in his dying. Bonhoeffer wrote:

> It is nothing else but our fellowship with Jesus Christ that leads us to the ignominious dying that comes in confession, in order that we may in truth share in his Cross. The Cross of Jesus Christ destroys all pride. We cannot find the Cross of Jesus if we shrink from going to the place where it is to be found, namely, the public death of the sinner. And we refuse to bear the Cross when we are ashamed to take upon ourselves the shameful death of the sinner in confession. In confession we break through to the true fellowship of the Cross of Jesus Christ.[4]

This death applies pointedly to those bound by a false image of wholeness. Just ask Ben, the pastor who tried to hide his part in his emotional adultery with Kim.

Ben benefited from the good, false self that he projected to others. Through confessing his sin, Ben underwent a slow death. Surrendering that good, false self was akin to losing a friend for Ben; it involved "letting go and grieving this false self, . . . a costly, lengthy process that requires giving up a whole way of looking at and living one's life."[5] Ben felt a profound nakedness, sensing the loss of the gleaming shame coat that had prevented him from being exposed as the sinner he was. But through that humiliation—"the final act of shaming"—Ben also came to experience "the Cross of Jesus as [his] rescue and salvation."[6] His old man died, but it was God who conquered him. Now Ben shares in the resurrection of Christ.

This brings us to the second death we die in confession. We must crucify not only the social saint but also the sin we have confessed.

DYING TO SIN

To confess sin means to die to the sin. In other words, confession signals the deeper work of repentance. In naming sin we also turn from it, releasing what is false to God.

We wait in that posture of nakedness before God and with others. We thus make room for his provision in our lives. With the help of his people, we begin to receive new life. He raises us up according to his way and through his means—the Spirit of resurrection.

This involves a holy hunger, one made possible by refusing the false "food" we have depended upon. Letting go can feel like a dying, especially when that meal has become a kind of lifeline to the soul. Falsehood can feed us. It can render us profoundly dependent upon its sweetness. And pain-filled in its absence.

The Father revealed the power of such deceptively tasty food to me in Denmark. I went for a walk in Copenhagen and came upon a beautiful, lush garden. It was protected by an elegant yet fiercely barbed fence. In spite of the waning sun, I entered the garden through its lone gate. The splendor of the grounds drew me deeper into the center of the garden. I approached a large stone monument, surrounded by profuse foliage, in full flower. The sights and smells were intoxicating.

Then I realized that I was in an upscale cemetery! The monument was in fact a tomb, as were the smaller displays of stone and bloom around it. Everything took on a slightly morbid cast. But the garden still captivated me, and so I stayed until I could no longer read the tombstones. The sun had set.

I made my way back to the gate—and to my horror realized that it was locked. The posts surrounding the entrance raised their spearlike heads in defiance. "Just try to get out!" they seemed to chide. I ran around the circumference of the garden but found no other way out.

I called out for help. No one responded. So I knew what I had to do—I had to scale the fence. I managed to pull my body over its slippery front, then, dangling precariously over its sharp ends, I hurled my body over the other side and dropped. I sustained several cuts, tore my clothes and had the wind knocked out of me. But I was out.

This experience reminded me of the deception of sin and the way out of it—the cross, through which we die to the sin. Our freedom cost Jesus his life. And it costs us the pleasures of sin.

Repentance is not always easy. It can feel like death. Resurrection is on its way, but en route we endure our own small crosses. Ask anyone who has given up a long-term relationship for Jesus' sake.

I recall a woman I met at a conference in Pasadena, California. She spent a long time grieving over her sins, which included a ten-year lesbian relationship. I prayed for her. Eventually she looked up and we spoke about her process of healing and how it had stopped when she started her same-sex affair. Now, she declared, was the time to resume the healing journey. And she knew that the cost included forsaking her lesbian relationship.

I recall her earnest, tear-stained face and confession. She knelt before the crucified One, dying in order to live. That day she grasped anew the relevance of the call to lose one's life in order to find it in Christ (Mt 10:39).

The cross bids us die. Our confession must initiate a decision to let go of the idol we have cherished. But the sacrifice is always worth it. Jesus promised, "No one who has left . . . brothers or sisters . . . for me and the gospel will fail to receive a hundred times as much in this present age . . . and in the age to come, eternal life" (Mk 10:29-30).

CONFESSION AND FORGIVENESS

The death we die as sinners in confession gives rise to new life. Something in fact has died—our social saint (more pernicious in some than others) as well as the power of the sin itself. But we become alive to Christ and his church as never before. We arise in Christ with the family of Christ. In the light of his resurrection, veils of shame, guilt and deception fall away, demons flee and sin's power begins to dissipate.

Forgiveness is the first expression of this resurrection power. Upon appearing to his disciples, the resurrected Christ sent out his disciples with the command to forgive sins. "He breathed on them and said, 'Receive the Holy Spirit. If you forgive anyone his sins, they are forgiven; if you do not forgive them, they are not forgiven' " (Jn 20:22-23). We as his disciples are thus imbued with his Spirit to proclaim forgiveness to those who confess sins. This is resurrection power, since the proclamation "You are forgiven, in Jesus' name" resurrects a person from the death of the sin.

Assurance of forgiveness results from a priestly proclamation. The brother or sister who has heard our confession speaks the word of forgiveness. Without such a witness, we are prone to mumbling admissions of sin and absolving ourselves, neither of which can impart the power of new life to us. Only the forgiveness of God can. And this occurs with certainty through the priestly word of our brother or sister.

Bonhoeffer wrote, "Who can give us the certainty that, in the confession and the forgiveness of our sins, we are not dealing with ourselves but with the living God? God gives us this certainty through our brother. . . . The assurance of forgiveness becomes fully certain to me only when it is spoken by a brother in the name of God. Mutual, brotherly confession is given to us by God in order that we may be sure of divine forgiveness."[7]

CONFESSION AND CHURCH COVERING

Through confession we break through to the cross and the community of the cross. This results in resurrection, understood as the certainty of God's forgiveness. Also the power of Christ's body is brought to bear upon our lives. Confession to others invites the authority of the church—against which hell cannot prevail (see Mt 16:18)—to empower us to stand uprightly against the sin.

While sin breaks down relationships, confession restores them. We can then join with Christ's community in our battle against sin. Through confession we become known. That knowing by a few representatives of the body frees us to receive ongoing prayer and care in our areas of greatest vulnerability. The world still beckons to us in powerful ways, but in the shelter God provides through our trusted family members we discover the more powerful stronghold that God has provided through his community.

This constitutes church covering: the ongoing relationships with people in our worshiping community to whom we confess sin and whom we enlist in the struggle against sin. The church has no mystical power to save us from sin unless we actively engage with her. This involves more than mere church attendance; it occurs through mutual submission to a handful of "priests" in that church with whom we become known as a sinner struggling to walk in freedom.

How crucial this connection is for individuals dealing with sexual and relational sins! These are failures that inflame foolish desires and frustrate our real needs. What remains is our yearning for love and connection, for belonging—that intrinsic desire to become a good gift to others. God in his infinite wisdom thus insists that we work out our sexual and relational brokenness within his body. He unites us with his raised body as we seek to emerge into sexual and relational wholeness, for relational problems require relational solutions.

The community of the cross has never been more needed as the cleansing, healing source for sexual and relational sinners. I've already referred to the desecration of God's image—humanity as male and female—in today's culture. We must take seriously the particular sins of which we each are guilty in this chain of destruction. Its beginning may be rooted in the garden, but we have all added to the momentum of sin outside of Eden.

TAKING RESPONSIBILITY

Taking responsibility for our sin is actually a great freedom. I cannot insist that another assumes his or her responsibility, but I can assume my own. This frees me to receive forgiveness and to act in new and responsible ways toward those around me.

To be sure, we need healing keys other than confession in our quest for wholeness. But confession of sin is primary. It gives us a choice. And it enables us to stand upright before the Father and to welcome the transforming power of grace. Our first priority and our fundamental freedom involve confessing our sin before God and trusted others.

We have much to confess. Because of the Fall, we are each subject to relational sins. These began immediately, as Adam and Eve covered themselves in their shameful nakedness, ceasing to love each other and their Creator in full. And then we are each heirs of this cover-up. We block and counter the other in our quest for relational security. We thus relate chaotically on a continuum from slavish devotion to detachment to cruelty.

In our fallenness lie the roots of our defensive, self-serving behaviors. These may or may not involve sexual sins. All sexual sins are relational, but not all relational sins are sexual. Relational sins are common to all humanity. To deny them is to deny that we are each creatures of the Fall.

OWNING RELATIONAL SINS

The fallen pair set in motion a struggle for power that has raged since time's beginning. Whereas in Eden they complemented one another in wholeness, outside of the garden the genders tend to merge in brokenness.

In the case of a woman, we see her greater relational capacity becoming a potential source of sin. She now yearns for a man's love inordinately—a tendency that places her at risk of making a god out of a mere mortal. This occurs when she allows herself to be subject to the broken creation in a manner that eclipses the primacy of the Creator in her life. From this flow the sins of a woman compromising her dignity to satisfy a man's cruel demands. Her idolatry is paired with the sin of self-hatred.

Many men reinforce this idolatry through requiring much of a woman and yet giving little. They want leadership without the cost of serving a woman in love. They may even justify the imbalance on the grounds that men are superior (usually a quietly though deeply held belief) and thus entitled to receive more than she does. This can lead to all manner of boorish, demeaning behaviors toward women. At its root such sin involves misogyny, or the hatred and dishonor of woman.

Modern women often tend toward a counterreaction to this traditional idolatry. A woman may ignore her need for men altogether. This is a posture of worldly justice; the woman now exists in reaction to the man's historic cruelty. She becomes larger than the man—more confident, more capable and free to need him no longer. In reaction to his abuses, she now refuses him. Her sin involves the suppression of her good and appropriate need for the man. She complements his misogyny with misandry, the hatred and dishonor of man.

Many men today grow up in a culture rife with misandry and misogyny. The battle for justice has resulted in evolving gender roles. This confusion, combined with a lack of adequate fathering, can leave men boyish and underdeveloped in their masculinity. They are thus prone to bonding with women in their immaturity.

Unsure of himself, this type of male does not lord himself over the woman in his life, but neither does he love her with the clarity and commitment that healthy relationships require. His presence may be underwhelming; hers, larger than life. She retains control through her greater function in the relationship and yet resents him for his littleness. Her disrespect reinforces his disempowerment. He remains at odds with himself and subject to self-contempt. She struggles for security in her oversized, maternal posture. Both need to confess the sins of not standing in their true adult status: man and woman before the Creator. Their mother-child dynamic undermines God's intent for his image bearers.

Related to this boyish immaturity is a pervasive theme I see in men today—the tendency toward narcissism. Here the man, unaffirmed and self-absorbed, engages the woman with a limited capacity to give himself to her. The relationship revolves around him. Even then he is nearly unable to love her, to extend himself beyond the awareness of his own desires. He sees her only to the degree that she satisfies him.

Such chronic selfishness can be cured only if it is acknowledged. Confessing the idolatry of self is the beginning of healing here. This requires more than the other party's suffering long. It must involve the clear witness that such a self-serving posture is wrong. Otherwise the one partner can contribute to the idolatry of the narcissistic other.

OWNING SEXUAL SINS

Sexual sin can be understood as a type of narcissism. It is inherently self-serving.

I had stayed up one night to watch a morally questionable TV show. To do so, I had to turn off any communication with Annette and my children. I wanted to escape into a painless, pleasurable world over which I had complete control. In confessing my sin to a friend later, I received these sobering words from him: "Your greatest sin, Andy, is not the pornography per se; it is the selfishness you exhibit in withholding yourself from your loved ones."

Sexual sins occur when we fail to do the hard work of forging a relationship and instead opt for the shortcut of sensual pleasure and release. Our sin may involve a person with whom we have no right to engage physically because we are not married to him or her. Or it may involve images of others with whom we bond through masturbation.

In either case, we fail to uphold the main premise of our sexuality—it is meant to be experienced only in the context of a committed, heterosexual relationship: marriage.

When we step outside of that context, sexually speaking, we subject ourselves to the destructive power of sin. We are unprotected. And we endanger others, like broken power lines lashing out in many directions. We ignite passions within ourselves and within others that cannot be satisfied. In the process we ignore our call to love others purely, in preparation for the one we will love faithfully in the entirety of his or her being.

Sexual sin is wrong because it causes us to reduce people to the sum of our lusts. It engenders self-absorption and betrays our holy commitments to God, self and others. On the more practical side, sexual sin creates immoral memories that we bear until heaven. (To say nothing of sexually transmitted diseases and unwanted pregnancies!) Sexual sin distorts the gift of our sexuality, that is, God's call for us to become a good gift to another. As such, broken sexuality undermines our relationships.

That's why Paul was powerfully clear in his exhortations against sexual immorality to the church at Thessalonica: "It is God's will that you . . . should avoid sexual immorality; that each of you should learn to control his own body in a way that is holy and honorable, not in passionate lust like the heathen, who do not know God; *and that in this matter no one should wrong his brother or take advantage of him.* The Lord will punish men for all such sins, as we have already told you and warned you" (1 Thess 4:3-6, emphasis added). Paul recognized the destructive power of sexual sin upon our relationships in the body of Christ. In its power, sexual sin causes us to wrong one another, to take advantage of a brother or sister.

This applies beyond obvious acts of adultery and seduction. Sexual immorality can be conceived through a computer screen. Young people today are barraged with graphic sexual images from the $8-billion-a-year pornography industry.[8] Through the Internet this foul industry is enslaving millions of young minds. Every day my teenagers are exposed to lewd advertisements from pornographic websites. The effect of such an assault can be a pernicious addiction that robs the soul of its dignity and sanctity. It also undercuts one's capacity to view others purely, since pornography so distorts perception that the "user" reduces those around him or her to players on the perverse screen of the mind. This is robbery of the highest order.

I cannot downplay the power of sexual images to invade the heart. God created us with a boundary around our imaginations and affections. When we visually ingest images of graphic sexuality, this protective wall is assaulted. If hit repeatedly, the wall breaks down. The unprotected heart (seat of our will, thoughts, emotions and memories) is soon dominated by perversion. And idolatry. These sexual images become little gods and goddesses to which we devote ourselves. We think about them, give our money and time to worship them, offer them our bodies and break covenant with real sources of love in order to pursue them.

Sex out of context renders us out of control. It causes us to worship other gods. Jeremiah cried out to his people, amid their spiritual and sexual idolatry, on God's behalf: "You have forgotten me and trusted in false gods [resulting in] adulteries and lustful neighings [and] shameless prostitution" (Jer 13:25-27). Paul recognized the same link between sexual immorality and false spirituality in the church at Corinth. There new Christians worshiped Jesus while at the same time having sex with temple prostitutes. The apostle thus implored them to flee fornication on the ground of their true calling—to honor God (and others) through single-hearted devotion to himself. "Do you not know that your body is a temple of the Holy Spirit, who is in you? . . . You are not your own; you were bought at a price. Therefore honor God with your body" (1 Cor 6:19-20).

Other expressions of sexual sin can be equally destructive but more subtle. Individuals in their loneliness can use others emotionally and physically. Sexual immorality can be conceived through emotionally adulterous relationships. These unions can be homosexual or hetero-sexual and often involve one party in a position of spiritual leadership. In such cases the sexual offense is compounded by the abuse of spiritual power. Here the pursuit of intimacy with Christ together becomes a partaking of one another. The holy embrace becomes romantic and arousing, the laying on of hands becomes sensual touch and the one who intended to keep his or her eyes fixed on Jesus begins to have eyes only for the other.

In such unions a participant often justifies the relationship on the grounds of not legally violating the other (for example, no intercourse takes place). But in actuality what has been conceived is outside the parameters of godly friendship. The heart, intended to be opened for spouses alone, receives the seemingly holy friend. The guardian of conscience is temporarily deceived. Powerful longings well up in the presence of the other and are satisfied.

Until the next fix, that is. One comes to need more of the other; he or she comes to depend upon the other like an infant upon its mother.

I recall one of my friendships that began to take more and more of my heart's attention. I was unaware of its danger. Then I began to realize that I was thinking more of this person than I was of Jesus or my wife. Annette came to me in fear and trembling to share a picture she had received from the Lord while praying. She saw me in my devotional time, with a large cross slightly above me. But instead of looking up to Jesus, I was looking at a small photograph below the cross. It was a picture of this friend. Busted! Her word of knowledge prompted a series of confessions and a slow dying that resulted in the restoring of protective boundaries around my dearest relationships, those with Jesus, Annette and my kids.

Sexual sin is profound and destructive. It robs all involved of the honor and pleasure God intends for us. As we seek to live out what it means to be sexual, stewarding our yearnings to not be alone (see Gen 2:18), we face real shortcuts to love and connectedness. Sexual sin is one such shortcut. Few of us are exempt from its powers of persuasion. The needs in our lives are great, and at times the power to make or to sustain a committed union is too hard for us in our weakness. At those times love outside of the boundaries, be it in fantasy or reality, can be hard to resist.

But resist it we must and we can. Consider the effect of such violations. For one thing, sexual sin grieves our Father. As a type of idolatry, it dishonors the Spirit within us as well as our own bodies. And it victimizes many people. Those who sin impact friends and lay a weak foundation for future faithfulness.

HATING OUR SEXUALITY

Often the most wounded ones are those who have been passed over by someone else who has chosen an illicit lover. Wounded spouses need a healing all their own. For some, their wounding in adult relationships began much earlier, through childhood sexual abuse. When joined with disappointing or wounding experiences in adulthood, these early sexual experiences may tempt a person to shut the door altogether on the good gift of sexuality. We need healing for those wounds.

But we also must do our part. We must uphold the truth that each of us remains a good gift to others. In spite of the damage done, we can stand with our Creator and trusted others in believing that the damage need not have the defining word on our sexuality. We begin by confessing the sin of our disavowal of the gift. This opens us to the healing grace we need to live out the truth that we are good gifts to others.

Sexual and relational sins come in many forms. But their cure always begins the same way—through confession in community. There we discover the cross of Christ. We enter through his threshold of death; we name our sin, and in surrendering it to the Lord, we die to it. And in the witness of forgiveness, through the gracious presence and blessing of our brother or sister, we rise again. We join with Christ in his new life, confident that the power of his transforming love has taken new ground in our hearts. Let me review the basic steps of this process.

STEPS OF CONFESSION

Confession is not necessarily a one-shot procedure. Instead it is a process; it unfolds.

First of all, we must seek out trustworthy "priests" in our faith communities. As an evangelical Protestant, I do not have a Roman Catholic priest as my "father." Nor do I have access to my senior pastor. (Many in larger churches do not.) But I do have access to trustworthy fellow believers who can hear my confession and support me in my recovery.

Sometimes a small-group leader is the best person for us to ask to hear our confession. At other times we can ask a godly friend to serve us in that way. Regardless of who it may be, we need to seek out such a person and enlist him or her as our prayer partner.

Having found a friendly priest, our next step is to tell him or her in plain terms what we have done wrong. No euphemism will do; this is the time to come clean. In speaking our sin out loud, we define the falsehood and take responsibility for it.

The confessional liberates us from the buffers of rationalization and dismissal, both of which usually occur in silence. In the presence of the priest we cannot view sin "with a dispersed mind, see something of it, see it in passing, see it with half-closed eyes, with a divided mind, see it and indeed not see it."[9] Through verbal expression before another, the sin comes into the light. It can now find its end on the cross.

Next, the priest binds the sin away from us and onto the cross. This is an application of the ministry of binding and loosing that Jesus gave his disciples (Mt 16:18-19). It can be helpful here to actually behold a cross. In the binding away of the confessed sin, its power is broken. A holy exchange has occurred. Jesus now bears the unbearable; he assumes the weight of sin as it is lifted off our shoulders and placed upon him.

A word here on the quickening of repentance through confession.

We can only give away what we decide we do not want. Jesus' assuming the weight of our sin means that we want to be rid of it. Our surrendering our sin to him means that we die to it; we choose to release it to him. He is willing to bear it, but we must let go of it in order for him to do so. The binding away of our sin thus highlights the call and necessity to surrender our sin.

To be sure, we may need to confess the same sin many times over before its domination in our lives is completely broken. This can be true of long-standing sins like sexual fantasy and masturbation. It is also true of deeply held attitudes like misogyny, self-hatred or selfishness. Still, the confession needs to be motivated by the desire to be free from the sin.

When that is the case, the binding away of the sin signals another holy assault upon the stronghold of the sin. Grace, truth and transforming power now have fresh access to our heart. There is more room for us to welcome God and his goodness into our lives. That empowers us to make better choices the next time a familiar temptation occurs.

Now we can approach sin on the unshakable ground of forgiveness. Our priest, after binding away the sin, looses forgiveness. The proclamation "You are forgiven!" is the language of resurrection. These three words convey the truth that God has released us from the guilt and shame of our sin. We are now free to stand before him and others uprightly, no longer bowed down by the weight of our sin. We can live with him now in the light of his victory over sin and death.

Forgiveness from sin accompanies the cleansing of that sin from our midst. The apostle John paired forgiveness and cleansing (1 Jn 1:9) and so must we. Sin stains the soul and body. We thus need to be cleansed from its destructive effects.

On the cross Christ released a flood of blood and water (Jn 19:34). I view the blood as the assurance of sin's dissolution and the water as the agent of washing away the effects of sin. Hebrews 10:22 refers to "having our hearts sprinkled to cleanse us from a guilty conscience and having our bodies washed with pure water." And Ezekiel prophesied that God would "sprinkle clean water" on a people bound by idolatry. Its effect would be to cleanse them from all of their impurities and idols (Ezek 36:25). That washing foretold the ultimate cleansing that Christ loosed at Calvary. Our priest may want to employ water as a symbol of that cleansing.[10]

After our priest has administered forgiveness and cleansing, he or she blesses us as one beloved of the Father and one belonging to his body, the church. This again underscores the value of corporate confession—the priest represents the church, to which one can now be knit in anew. Sin breaks fellowship; confession restores it. Our priestly friend thus administers the blessing of our belonging that closes the gap left by the sin itself. He or she may also offer particular words of encouragement and healing. As confession exposes our failures, we need to be covered afresh by the kindness and tenderness of the saints.

Real covering by Christ's body in areas where we struggle against darkness demands ruthless honestly. And continuity with the same priests. As I battled with pornography, Jesus said something to me that I will never forget: "Do not pray to me for freedom unless you are willing to confess your sin!" This required many confessions to the same people. Ultimately God enabled me to overcome my sin. The key was confession to his body, "the pillar and foundation of the truth" (1 Tim 3:15). Becoming founded on that truth requires confession in community.

Following the blessing, our priest may want to lead us to renounce the sin of which we have been forgiven. This is key to breaking long-standing sin patterns. As an act of our will, we take authority over that sin. We are a favored and freshly empowered child of the Father; we stand in and with the community against which hell cannot prevail. In that authority we renounce the power of sin in the greater power granted us in Christ. This is an application of Paul's multiple exhortations to put to death the deeds of the flesh (Gal 5:24; Eph 4:22-24; Col 3:5-10).

Many of us are not fighters by nature, but we must do our part in the battle against sin. We thus need to be trained alongside our priests to refuse sin and its overtures. Since our entering the confessional, the world has not become more holy for our sakes. But we have. And we can arise and go forward with a new freedom to walk in the authority Jesus has won for us through his cross and community—the power of confession.

UNCOVERING OUR WEAKNESSES

When we confess, Jesus raises us up in his powerful mercy. Reclaimed by the truth, "we have renounced secret and shameful ways; . . . nor do we distort the word of God. On the contrary, by setting forth the truth plainly we commend ourselves to every man's conscience in the sight of God" (2 Cor 4:2). We in our sin and shame have endured "the final shaming" through the cross discovered in confession. Truth and grace replace sin as the stronghold in our lives.

Confession is the way to strength in weakness. For those of us morally vulnerable in any direction—subject to a variety of temptations to not love well—our naming sin and receiving forgiveness opens us to the inexhaustible resource of Christ's power. His blood has removed the veil of sin and shame. Our weakness remains—the vulnerability to sin. Now uncovered by sin and shame, we invite the transforming strength of his grace into our weakness.

6

WOUNDS THAT HEAL

I recall a time when I was overcome by the failure of certain colleagues. My capacity to rise up and to do something to displace the pain failed me. I sat and wept before the cross. After a while, though, I could hear the still, small voice of God say, "I am inviting you to share in my suffering, my pain of rejection and abandonment." With that word came more tears and an easing of the pain. Most importantly, it showed me the value of slowing down amid wounding and disappointment in order to meet the Lord in suffering.

Pain acknowledged before God invites deeper communion with him. Were I to deny my pain through much activity, I would deny myself the healing that comes only with allowing him to bear my suffering. Joining with Christ on the occasion I have described freed me to rise with him. I had faced the truth of the suffering at hand. I could then proceed with a sober awareness of the Lord's presence and control as I arose in his greater life.

The cross is central here. We have already identified how the cross breaks the power of shame and bears our sins, allowing us to become good gifts to others. But the wounds we bear through others' sins against us can entomb us as readily as can bad shame or impurity. We thus need to know how to identify our wounds, to give ourselves time to feel our pain and to allow Christ to assume our suffering.

The crucified God draws near to the forsakenness of every man and woman. As Jürgen Moltmann has said, "There is no loneliness and no rejection which he has not taken to himself and assumed in the cross of Jesus."[1]

IDENTIFYING OUR WOUNDS

I find this dimension of healing more difficult to deal with than confession of shame or sin. Somehow confession, especially the confession of personal sin, affords me more control. I did something wrong and thus I confess it. But to acknowledge the chaotic, unpredictable nature of my reactions to another's failure—this is a greater challenge. That's because I am reminded of how vulnerable I am as one connected to someone who is capable of failing me.

We fallen ones do not love well! To face wounding is to stand naked in one's neediness; it is to reenter the truth that one hurts only because one has loved. We took up the call to community—to become a good gift for others—only to discover that others are as capable of withholding goodness as they are of giving it.

The pathway to love and trust in a fallen world is perilous. En route we have a choice: we can either submit our suffering to Christ or we can harden our hearts. The latter may be our greatest temptation, as self-protection lures us more powerfully than do bold acts of vengeance or seduction. We want to rebuild the defensive wall behind which we have lived most of our lives. Yet unless we learn to face and express our pain, it may express itself in destructive ways.

I experienced this profoundly during a conference recently. Many had gathered to face a variety of sexual and relational problems, including a slew of addictions. During the speaker's talk on the value of facing pain, I sensed a deep well of unexpressed pain in the room. The conferees were mindful of their sin but were not as clear about the suffering underneath it. Before inviting people forward for the ministry time, I tried to articulate this as best I could.

The response was astounding. The people wailed before the cross as Jesus freed their hearts to express pent-up pain. We grieved together for nearly an hour. I believe we were weeping as representatives of a generation more intent on enjoying pleasure and prosperity than on facing the pain of our lives. As a result we were better able to proceed soberly in pursuit of God's good will and purpose for our lives.

Jesus always helps us face the pain of our lives. And as he does so, he draws us closer to himself. The apostle Paul provided a clear witness to the powerful role of hardship in identifying with Christ.

PAUL AND PAIN

In an earlier chapter I referred to the significant trials Paul faced and articulated to the Corinthians. In addition to his "thorn in the flesh" (a significant personal struggle we cannot identify), Paul suffered due to a variety of pressures, troubles and distresses. He did not shy away from expressing these afflictions. Rather, he claimed that in such suffering he identified with Christ and partook of his comfort. The result was comfort that overflowed to the Corinthians (2 Cor 1:5-7).

Paul's distresses resulted from his apostolic mission. He was not suffering due to his own foolishness but rather due to the resistance he faced in advancing the gospel. We can say confidently that Paul suffered for what was right.

This reminds us that we must seek to distinguish among the sources of our pain. When we suffer because of bad choices we make, we do not want to spiritualize our suffering as "the suffering of Christ." Rather, we should seek forgiveness for these bad choices and ask for the wisdom to learn from our mistakes.

But at times we will suffer due to others' sin. As Christians seeking to do right, we will sustain wounds from the faithful and faithless. We can then discover the holy advocacy Paul described in 2 Corinthians. Like Paul, we can present our wounds to Christ as the ground for holy suffering and comfort.

Paul began the letter by boldly expressing the weakness he felt in his wounding. In truth he felt despair and "the sentence of death" (1:9). We later hear of multiple threats to his well-being due to persecution and the pressure of church-related concerns (11:23-28). He lamented, "This body of ours had no rest, but we were harassed at every turn—conflicts on the outside, fears within" (7:5). Paul suffered at the hands of many and endured much antagonism. He was not afraid of expressing the suffering he faced as he sought to advance the gospel.

Such expression of suffering gave Paul a chance to preach the whole truth to the church in Corinth. Other so-called Christian leaders tempted the Corinthians with a cross-free faith born of human wisdom and power. In his suffering, though, Paul identified with and proclaimed the suffering God. And at the same time Paul proclaimed that the Christ who had been crucified had also been raised and in turn would deliver him from his death sentence (1:9-10).

Throughout his letters Paul helps us to understand that suffering this side of heaven is to be expected. In fact, that suffering is a prerequisite of being a true son or daughter of the Father. Paul put a condition on his claim that we are God's children, saying we are Christ's heirs "if indeed we share in his sufferings in order that we may also share in his glory" (Rom 8:17).

To know Christ involves identifying with him in the hardship and the joy of following him. By sharing in his suffering, we gain a share in the resurrection. Paul definitively stated that in Philippians 3:10-11: "I want to know Christ and the power of his resurrection and the fellowship of sharing in his sufferings, becoming like him in his death, and so, somehow, to attain to the resurrection from the dead."

Let us expect suffering then. Let us not fear pain but accept it as a condition of living as human beings this side of heaven. But as Christian human beings, we can face our pain before the One who heals our wounds. His authority to heal us lies in his endurance of intense suffering and his triumph over that suffering through his resurrection. The cross thus represents at once the God who entered into our misery and the reign of glory that alleviates our misery.

Let's look next at how Christ combines both sympathy and healing power for us in our suffering.

JESUS AND PAIN

Sin causes suffering; it sets up a chain reaction of disorder and death. This includes, at a basic level, the suffering that we sustain as a result of others' sin against us. Jesus' assuming the weight of sin applies to our own transgressions as well as to the wounds inflicted on us by others. Thus the Suffering Servant bears our sorrows and grief (Is 53:4). This pertains to the emotion tied to losses and lacerations we sustain in our relationships.

Jesus' assuming human suffering also reflects on his own experience of suffering. Prior to his death on the cross, Jesus endured profound humiliation. This included cruelty at the hands of political authorities (the Roman officials) and religious leaders (the Pharisees and the Sanhedrin). Their opposition to Christ intensified as his influence grew and culminated in their crucifying him. In preparation for his death these men mocked, slapped, spit on and whipped the captive Lamb.

But for Jesus, the abandonment of his friends provoked a far greater suffering than did the cruelty of the political and religious authorities. His disciples, in whom Jesus had invested many months of training and who had pledged their allegiance to him, failed to sustain their commitment to him. This was clearly demonstrated when Jesus at Gethsemane grew "sorrowful and troubled." He said to his disciples, "My soul is overwhelmed with sorrow to the point of death. Stay here and keep watch with me" (Mt 26:37-38). Christ implored them to abide with him in his suffering as he reflected upon the agony ahead on the cross. They could not stay awake for even an hour with him (v. 40). Then, at his arrest, "all the disciples deserted him and fled" (v. 56).

The Savior has entered into human suffering ever since the rejection, abuse and abandonment he endured from people prior to his crucifixion. But that wounding was a mere preface to the horror that awaited him on the cross. This included a slow, agonizing death as he was strung up naked before a jeering crowd. In crucifixion the dying God was raised up to be publicly humiliated. His nail-pierced hands, feet and side stung him, as did the crown of thorns that mocked his claim to divinity. Of these scars Thomas Smail writes, "The uniqueness of Jesus is not in the loftiness of his teaching, the immaculate holiness of his life, the supernatural power of his miracles . . . but rather in his scars, in his sharing in our sufferings."[2]

In this suffering God chose to reveal himself as One who suffers, who enters into the misery of our sin in order to break its grip. Moltmann said, "The God of freedom, the true God, is therefore not recognized by his power and glory in the world . . . but through his helplessness and his death [in] the scandal of the cross of Jesus."[3] He continued, "God is not greater than he is in this humiliation. God is not more glorious than he is in this self-surrender. God is not more powerful than he is in this helplessness. God is not more divine than he is in this humanity."[4] God reveals himself in the utter vulnerability of the crucified Christ.

His ultimate agony awaited him. As men withdrew their support, Jesus placed his hope in the Father all the more. As he bore the weight of sin's burden, his reliance upon his heavenly Father increased.

GRIEF OF FATHER AND SON

Imagine Jesus' dismay, as recorded in the Gospels, when the darkness of sin overshadowed him and barred him from access to the Father. This was his supreme abandonment. The Son, whose life on earth consisted of unflagging obedience to his Father, could not find the Father at his moment of greatest need. That veil of sin separated the Son from the Father.

As the darkness fell upon the dying Son, the Father turned away from him (Mt 27:45-46). Jesus expressed a profound abandonment by the Father with loud cries and tears (Heb 5:7). Almost his last cry was the lament of abandonment: "My God, my God, why have you forsaken me?" (Mk 15:34). Then sin extinguished the life of the Son.

In his dying the Suffering Servant assumed the penalty of sin, paying it in full. Jesus knew this as he cried out just prior to his death, "It is finished" (Jn 19:30). At the same time his awareness of completing the payment in no way minimized his experience of forsakenness.

God abandoned God. The meaning of this for us is profound as we consider how Christ shares our suffering, including the suffering of abandonment. We must understand this abandonment as twofold, first in the experience of the Son and then in the experience of the Father.

Jesus' unique fellowship with the Father in his life sheds light upon his abandonment in death.[5] Jesus lived as one alive to the grace-filled God who drew near to him, leading him every step toward the cross. And thus we can begin to understand his agony of forsakenness on the cross. "It is the experience of abandonment by God in the knowledge that God is not distant, but close. . . . And this, in full consciousness that God is close at hand in his grace, to be delivered and abandoned up to death as one rejected, is the torment of hell."[6]

But did Jesus alone experience this torment? A superficial reading of Isaiah 53:10—"It was the LORD's will to crush him and cause him to suffer"—could give the impression that the Father subjected the Son to suffering but himself remained aloof from it. Not so! Christ's agony was, I believe, matched by the suffering of the Father.

On behalf of humanity's sin sickness, the Father suffered the loss of his Son. His grief in subjecting his Son to such humiliation and abandonment corresponds with the grief of the Son in his forsakenness. Moltmann wrote, "The Son suffers dying, the Father suffers the death of the Son. The grief of the Father here is just as important as the death of the Son. The Fatherlessness of the Son is matched by the Sonlessness of the Father."[7]

Yet the Father's grief was different from the Son's grief. Christ was bewildered in his abandonment and thus appealed to the Father, "Why?" The Father, on the other hand, knew what the Son had to endure, and perhaps that foreknowledge added to his agony. He knew that the Son would be cut off from him; how else could he wholly assume sin and pay its penalty? The Father's decision to allow his Son to endure such suffering meant the grief of subjecting his beloved One to abandonment.

The grief of both the Father and Son in the cross is crucial to our understanding of the God who suffers on our behalf. The Father initiated the abandonment of Christ unto sin and death, and the Son obeyed. The two are united in their love for humanity in its sin sickness, so much so that they allowed themselves to be subject to the ultimate agony—the Father's abandonment of the Son. In that suffering, one far more intense than Christ's suffering at the hands of men, the Father and the Son revealed their unfathomable love for us. The two endured the grief of abandonment and loss for us, the sin-sick and forsaken.

HOLY EMPATHY AND POWER

God entered into our plight—our griefs and abandonment. God thus beckons to us with holy empathy. Emily Dickinson wrote, "When Jesus tells us about his Father, we distrust him, when he shows us his Home, we turn away, but when he confides to us that he is 'acquainted with Grief,' we listen, for that also is an Acquaintance of our own."[8] The losses we sustain, often arbitrary and inexplicable and revealing new depths of pain to us, may very well be the points of greater intimacy with the God who suffers.

But while the cross reveals divine empathy, it also displays holy power. Calvary signifies a point of exchange where suffering is replaced by joy. God empathizes with us in our suffering and he shoulders it with us unto holy release. The boundless love that proceeds "from the grief of the Father and the dying of the Son" possesses the power to reach forsaken men and women and to create in them "the possibility and the force of new life."[9]

Isaiah prophesied of the wounds that heal (Is 53:5). This refers to the power of Jesus' suffering, now swallowed up in the victory of his resurrection. The suffering of abandonment, common to sin-sick humanity, is overcome by the suffering of love. Jesus assumed what is sick and stinging upon himself. His wounds are magnetic; they invite us to place our wounds—griefs, losses, injuries, suffering of whatever kind—into his wounds. And so Christ imparts the holy comfort that Paul extolled as the first fruit of suffering in Christ's name (2 Cor 1:5).

Let us not make the mistake of those who extol an imbalanced mysticism of the cross. These emphasize the Son's suffering to the exclusion of his resurrection. Much as I respect many of these mystical writers, I resist the theology of Christ's "dark night" of suffering as a way of life for Christians. God does allow us to endure suffering, but I challenge the notion that he withholds himself from us amid the suffering. He avails himself to us there in the power of his suffering and resurrection. He grants us holy comfort amid suffering.

Jesus is alive. The grave could not hold him, nor need our suffering this side of heaven contain us. Nothing need block the light emanating from the empty cross. For Paul and for us, the crucified Lord is always the resurrected Lord. God avails freely his new life to those who cleave to the cross in their dark night. Heed the brilliance of resurrection; its constant light must inform our identification with the suffering God. There we discover the divine empathy that woos us in our devastation, urging us to lay our burdens down at the feet of the crucified, then raises us up once more with the power of his comfort and new life.

KEYS TO THE WOUNDS THAT HEAL

There are three components to this exchange of our wounds for Christ's healing. The first is participating in community—others who bear with us in our suffering. The second is waiting for his release to come, learning how to bear suffering. The third is being willing to forgive those who have wounded us.

I have witnessed the relevance of these principles time and time again for those who have been severely wounded by others. All of them were well demonstrated in the life of a woman named Julie.

Julie came to Annette and me a while ago to request prayer for her marriage. Her normally steady Christian husband had begun acting strangely. He seemed remote, had stopped going to church and had become lax toward the family, lifting the basic family rules that had previously governed them. A few months after our prayer for Julie, he walked out on her and their three children, giving no reason except for a profound disillusionment and refusing any prospect of reconciliation.

The husband then battled Julie over finances, refusing to adequately support the family. After a while, the truth of his affair with another woman emerged. His girlfriend and her child moved in with him, even though for financial reasons he denied having a relationship with the woman.

Julie was floored. She had not been aware of any significant trouble in the marriage. They had struggles like everyone, but except for her husband's disappointment in certain areas of his life, their relationship seemed intact.

On top of her shock that evolved into grief, Julie did not know how to manage the household without her husband. He had carried the financial responsibility. So his abandonment of the family had weighty practical implications. The question of how to endure emotionally was matched by the question of how to pay the bills.

Deeper still was fear. Julie's parents had both deserted her—one through an early death, the other through alcoholism. She carried the threat of being abandoned throughout her adulthood. Now her worst fear had been realized in her husband's desertion of the family. Without him as her anchor, she was set adrift and terrified.

Julie suffered as never before. It was hard for her even to get out of bed. This was true of her children as well. One child became severely depressed, while another expressed his pain in drugs and various acts of hostility. The youngest was simply set adrift in confusion. The family was in chaos.

Prior to this time, Julie's strength had come more from her husband and from her devotion to God than from fellowship outside the home. But this season was different. Julie knew that in order to lead her family through their most difficult hour—the one in which pain was a constant, unrelenting presence—she needed to rely upon others as never before.

Julie discovered four people around her on whom she could rely for practical help and advice as well as a listening ear when she wanted to cry out from her heart. These were the ones who became the presence of Jesus for her. Other friends wanted to help, but due to her weakness and sense of shame, it was all Julie could do to expose herself to the four.

Julie's tears and rage, her experience of abandonment and forsakenness, became an offering. She extended this offering in different forms and degrees of intensity to God and her friends. In so doing, she met Jesus on the cross. Others stood with her as she grieved the loss at hand and presented her wounds to be healed. Jesus became her friend in suffering. She could not do much more than meet him in her distress.

Jesus beckoned to Julie as he did to his disciples in his agony, "Stay here and keep watch with me." Julie, in her suffering, learned to respond to the One who also had been overwhelmed with sorrow to the point of death. Like Paul, whose pressures were as a sentence of death (2 Cor 1:9), Julie cleaved to Christ in her abandonment. She learned to suffer with him.

In the past Julie had relied upon Christ in times of trouble. But those were, in contrast, temporary trials that were more like tremors than an earthquake. This time the suffering continued. She learned to wait before Christ in a posture of active suffering. Instead of descending into despair, she allowed herself to weep and rage—she poured out her heart. Thus her suffering could find an end in Christ, often with the help of her friends.

A wise man wrote of this process of active suffering, "Instead of yielding to despair, I chose the part of active melancholy, in so far as I possessed the power of activity, in other words I preferred the melancholy that hopes and aspires and seeks, to that which despairs in stagnation and woe."[10]

Julie, in her suffering, aspired to the hope of Christ, the bright light shining on the cross of her abandonment. Still, this unloading was a process. She learned to abide with Christ in pain. Each time she offered her pain to him, she met the God of all comfort, but that comfort did not displace the suffering. It seemed as if daily there were new and dark developments in her children, in her finances and in the bewildering revelation of this husband she thought she knew. And with each new occurrence, she struggled and then surrendered afresh to Christ. She grieved and she cried out to him to bear the new burden. He did.

Julie began to discover a truth that we all must if we are to be free to live in Christ this side of heaven. Jesus does not guarantee us a life free from suffering. Rather, he teaches us to suffer in and with him. In that way he becomes our comfort and our hope as never before.

Julie discovered amid her pain that she had never known such intimacy with Christ. She could say with the novelist Alan Paton, "I have never thought that a Christian would be free of suffering. . . . For our Lord suffered. And I [came] to believe that he suffered, not to save us from suffering, but to teach us how to bear suffering."[11] Julie learned in this process how to bear suffering with Christ—and how to rise with him into new life.

Key to Julie's resurrection was the choice to forgive her wounders. Julie already knew what the Bible teaches about forgiveness, but she had never been betrayed as she was by her husband. The challenge to forgive was the greatest she had yet faced. But God gave her the grace and the courage to release him again and again as new dimensions of his darkness cast their shadow on her.

She forgave him for Jesus' sake and through his power. But she also forgave for the sake of her own and the family's welfare. She simply could not secure a job and sort out the future without her husband while tethered to hatred and bitterness. The consequences of not forgiving him were too great, so she obeyed Christ in the power of his resurrection when he empowered the disciples to forgive (Jn 20:20-

23). She experienced a freedom to act through the binding away of her husband's sin of abandoning them via the choice to forgive him.

New life became evident to Julie and her family after about two years. Each child found healing and hope. The pain subsided for Julie. She began to accept her situation and to rejoice in her strengthened muscle of faith. Most importantly, she is freer than ever to know Christ in his suffering and in his resurrection. Her wounding and healing have served her well. She is more empowered than ever to do God's will.

FACING EARLY WOUNDS

Let's look at some of the ways we can apply the power of the cross to our wounding. We will look first at some of the relational wounds we sustain early in life. These can influence certain tendencies we may develop toward sexual and relational brokenness. Recognizing these early influences can alert us to where we can apply the power of the cross. In this way God's strength can anchor us in our weaknesses and prevent those weaknesses from dominating us. Understanding our wounds, and the cross's relevance to them, frees us to love others with a whole heart.

I want to stress three key points here. First, we are all creatures of the Fall. We each receive a blessed and a broken inheritance from our families of origin. We must learn to identify some of the themes that comprise our inheritance without idealizing or demonizing others. Second, no one makes us sin. We choose the broad path of destruction for ourselves, though our wounding may contribute to our bad choices. Third, our individual personalities are a gift at birth that can be modified but not fundamentally altered over the course of a lifetime. Our personalities provide a grid though which we perceive and process the relational influences around us.

With those three points in mind, we can nevertheless hardly overestimate the role that parents play in our emergence as male and female. Through strong and affirming relationships with us, our parents invite us to accept our own gender while welcoming the other as a blessed complement to our own. On the other hand, broken relationships with either parent can hinder our ability to make peace with the call to bear God's image as male and female.

Both the same-sex parent and the opposite-sex parent play important roles for a child. Let's look first at the impact of the same-sex parent. The relationship with this parent is the lifeline to a child, securing a whole-enough sense of a boy as male or a girl as female.

THE SAME-SEX PARENT

Our same-sex parent is the main model of who we are becoming in our gender identities. Something primitive in us is designed to bond with, and to seek to emulate, this representation of manhood or womanhood. The same-sex parent most nearly represents the expression of male or female that we are designed to become.[12]

How badly we need this lifeline! When the lifeline is severed, the child is placed at a disadvantage. From whom will he or she receive gender role-modeling if not from the same-sex parent? Some seem to have an easier time than others finding sources for modeling outside the family, such as in sports, at church, and so on. But others seem to become blocked in their capacity to reattach to same-sex models.

Often, when the parental lifeline is severed through abuse, neglect, illness, death, divorce—anything that removes the parent from the child for a lengthy time period—the child may instinctively bar the parent in self-protection. This psychological device is called "defensive detachment."[13] We defend ourselves through erecting an unseen but real wall in relationship to the offender. As adults, we can be aware of this habit. But as children, particularly in early childhood, we can detach without being aware of what we are doing.

Defensive detachment in the child causes him or her to resist the parent. I saw this firsthand after an international ministry trip my wife and I took together when my daughter Katie was about one year old. We entrusted her to my mother-in-law's good care. But when Annette returned, Katie resisted Annette; the little one sought refuge elsewhere. It took her three days to welcome Annette's care again. Women we have worked with have experienced a similar defense as children, only more significant due to lengthy separation from the mother due to illness or death.

When this detachment toughens in relation to the same-sex parent, the child's gender security can be threatened. In some cases the child can make vows against the parent and who the parent represents—a more powerful image of the child as male or female. This causes him or her to resist good expressions of same-sex identification outside of the parent-child relationship.

I witnessed this clearly in my friend Sam's life. He was an intelligent and sensitive son of an illegal Latin immigrant in Los Angeles. They grew up poor. His alcoholic father belittled Sam for any expressions of weakness. In spite of the father's efforts at making his son a success in sports, Sam remembered only the physical and emotional battering he received from his father when he failed.

After a while, Sam's fear of his dad turned to hatred. He detached from everything about him. This made it nearly impossible for Sam to attach to gender role models in the barrio. He saw most Latino men through the lens of his abuse. This blocked his capacity to make peace with his ethnicity, his gender identity and his sexuality. He sought masculine connection through dependent relationships with upwardly mobile white men, which led him into the gay community of Los Angeles.

That sensual world of illusion and gender insecurity led Sam to cry out for mercy. Sam met a strong Christian who introduced him to Jesus. He thus began the journey of discovering the Father's love and the healing of his identity as a man.

A breakdown in relation to the same-sex parent always has an impact, but it affects people differently. What for Sam became a homosexual struggle may become for another a broken expression of heterosexuality.

Becky, for example, defended herself from a cold, demanding mother by detaching herself as a child. Her sexuality emerged normally but was fueled by an intense longing for love, not unlike that of an infant for its mother. Becky sought a binding emotional attachment with her husband, but that relationship could not satisfy. Neither could Becky's relationships with her girlfriends. She needed much attention, of a caliber that proved exhausting to those from whom she sought love.

Unlike many women whose dependencies are sexual, Becky did not possess a homosexual struggle. She was simply vulnerable to needing too much from either gender. She needed healing for the profound "mother wound" and detachment she had sustained for years.

Along the same lines, God effected a profound healing for me in regard to my father. He was loving yet unavailable at certain points in my childhood. Due to his lack of presence, and for other reasons, I detached from him and identified more closely with women than with men.

I felt many things toward my father, including contempt. But close to that contempt was the self-hatred I felt toward my own manhood. As I was at odds with my father's masculinity, so I was also at odds with my own.

During a particular healing season, God was faithful to bring up many of my judgments toward my father. In pain I brought them before Christ. The relational barrier between my father and me was clearly my own; it was comprised of lots of little wounds and my own bitter response to him. But Jesus bore my sin-sickness and I was able to forgive my father from a deep place in my heart, thus making a way for reunion with him.

A few months later I had a dream. I saw a block of stone out of which two sculpted torsos were emerging, close to each other and slightly different, though both clearly joined in the same stone base. I could see that the images were my father and me. We were united in our masculinity, intimately joined yet without a hint of perversion. We both looked strong and noble.

I awoke and rejoiced in the clear interpretation of the dream. I was and am my father's son. I bear his natural likeness irrevocably, as we were both hewn from the same stone. In making peace with my father, I was freed to accept both him and myself in our masculinity. The healing continues to this day as I seek to love and honor my father more.

THE OPPOSITE-SEX PARENT

Until we receive healing for wounds in relation to our same-sex parent, we will struggle to love the opposite gender freely and well. But even then we must face the impact of the opposite-sex parent. He or she is key to the image we hold toward the opposite gender. A clear and affirming relationship with that parent empowers us to behold the good of our gender counterpart. On the other hand, a broken union with the opposite-sex parent will hinder our freedom to love the other uprightly.[14]

The opposite-sex parent has unique authority to convey our adequacy and our dignity in relation to the opposite sex. This naturally impacts our capacity to relate in a whole heterosexual way. For example, a father who treasures his daughter will contribute to her sense of self-worth in relation to the other men in her life.

One day my daughter came home from school exasperated at the foolishness of her twelve-year-old peers. "Why are some girls willing to do such weird things to get a guy's attention?" she asked, referring to the sexy clothes and seductive actions of some girls. For her, a built-in sense of self-worth precluded such compromising behavior.

Bill's parents loved him but barely tolerated each other. His dad had an affair years before Bill was born, and Bill's mother had never forgiven her husband. With her anger, she became stronger and her partner became more passive. Bill repeatedly witnessed the power of his mother's tongue lacerating her husband. The father would just bear this treatment, as if bound to an endless cycle of penance. The mother confided in Bill about her pain, urging him to not be the kind of man his father was. Meanwhile, Bill's dad was either silent or absent for progressively longer periods of time.

All this had a profound impact on Bill in relation to women. He resisted strong women, fearing their strength would expose and overpower him. At the same time he felt unsure of his ability to lead in relation with women. So he took the lonely path of avoidance—he refused to engage with women intimately. This continued until he decided to face his pain and anger toward his parents at the foot of the cross. It was a struggle for him to admit the suffering he bore as a result of his parents' sick marriage. But he began to arise as a man who knew he did not need to repeat the failures of his family in relation to the opposite sex.

Our relationships with our parents matter, helping to determine the kind of man or woman we will be in our adult relationships. Also important are the kinds of opposite-sex relationships our parents modeled. Was there commitment? Demonstration of respect, honor and dignity? Honest resolution of conflict? Or was heterosexuality unsafe, degrading, wounding, not worth the cost of trying? We develop an inner picture of heterosexual intimacy through our exposure to our parents. As each of our childhood homes is broken to some degree—at once a glimpse of God's order and of sin's sickness—we enter into our adult relationships in need of healing.

Such healing is possible. But before proclaiming afresh the relevance of the cross to our relational healing, I want to say a word about abuse and its impact.

SEXUAL ABUSE

One should never dismiss the impact of abuse on a child. It has the power to destabilize a young life, even crippling the person's capacity to love and trust others as an adult. Simply put, child abuse occurs when an adult destructively uses his or her power against a child. Such misuse of power can be physical, emotional or sexual.[15] Sexual abuse is especially relevant to the subject of this book, and it is part of larger cultural trends that influence relational and sexual brokenness.

Over the last several decades we have witnessed a breakdown of boundaries, sexually speaking. No longer is sexual behavior contained within the walls of heterosexual marriage; it has spread out, first into the realm of consenting adults, then into the minds and hearts of millions through the media and the Internet. The gates around our imaginations and our bodies have been burned down through the idolizing of sexual freedom in our culture.

The impact of such idolatry on our children is enormous. Are they not the real victims of dad's carelessly misplaced *Playboy?* Children will always be those most adversely impacted by broken boundaries. This applies pointedly to those who are themselves targeted by abusers. My wife was one such victim.

One Christmas Eve a visiting relative broke into her four-year-old world and raped her. While her parents and extended family slept, he nearly smothered her in a grotesque effort to have intercourse with her. Afterward the abuser told her that she would die if she told anyone. She held the secret in for twenty-four years, refusing to deal with the incident. It was not until she felt safe enough in relation to me that she began to deal honestly with her abuse.

Annette had many symptoms of abuse, some of which God was faithful to heal even before she was ready to face the event itself. She had suffered all her life with panic attacks, an eating addiction (big people don't get abused) and psychosomatic disorders like skin rashes and colitis. She was afraid to give herself to another. Control was easier than the risk of love. At the same time she would sabotage opportunities for success. Of course many of these symptoms were linked to other influences as well, but at the very least, the abuse had seared her soul with the message "Your world is not safe."

Annette needed profound healing. God chose the season in which she could walk through that healing. This is key to remember. We do not delve into dark periods in our life alone or merely at the provocation of others. We do so when we are ready, when we are capable of facing the pain. This involves the presence of consistent, trusted others. Annette was ready. She wanted to face her fears for her own sake, for the sake of our marriage and also for the sake of our yet-unborn children.

We began to pray for Annette within the context of a small group of trusted friends and healers. There we invited Jesus to meet Annette in her injury. He was faithful to shine the light of his healing presence upon her at her most vulnerable point. His love for Annette at the point of her abuse freed her to feel the pain. That, combined with the love of her friends, gave her the courage to suffer forthrightly and redemptively.

Her intense grief lasted several weeks. We prayed for her often in that time. She accepted the yoke of emotional heaviness as part of the process, but with each round of tears, she released more to Christ.

She also needed to renounce certain themes that she had embraced almost instinctively after the abuse. The main one involved control. Annette possessed a stronghold of control, becoming bigger, smarter and angrier before others in order to not be victimized again. This even had demonic implications.

She raged against the need to renounce self-management of her situation. "If I do not control my own reality, I will only be injured again!" she insisted. Yet God gave Annette the courage to refuse her own self-defense and to entrust her little wounded self to Christ and his control. Her "big self" went down hard. But she emerged lighter, freer, more tuned in to God than to her own self-preserving instincts. At the end of this healing time Annette freely chose to forgive her abuser as well as her parents for unwittingly subjecting her to him. Forgiveness sealed that season of healing for her.

The implications of her healing for our relationship and family were huge. Previously I was tempted to feel as if I were the wounded one in the relationship—Annette was strong and confident; I, less so. But I began to see how some of Annette's strength was rooted in wounding. Thus as I stood in God's healing power on her behalf, she could become more yielding and my manhood could become more pronounced. She grew softer as I did my part; she found that she could rely on me in ways she had previously relied on herself.

The timing for all of this was inspired. Annette became pregnant and gave birth to our first son, Gregory. She embraced the uniquely feminine yearning to pull away from the demands of the outside world in order to make a home for little Greg.

ALL ARE WOUNDED

We sustain many different wounds in our lives, beginning in childhood. I have emphasized in this last section a few of the wounds rooted in our early relationships that can affect our relational capacity later on. I would be remiss, however, if I did not include the many ways that we sustain wounding in our adult relationships.

The healing of memories need not extend back several decades. We are wounded daily as we experience the slings and arrows of everyday life. This especially occurs with those we love the most. Strangers can hurt us, but their lacerations are skin-deep in contrast to those who have won, and then have betrayed, our trust.

When this occurs, we each have a choice. We can either get bigger and bitter in our resolve to not get wounded again or we can go the way of the cross. We have an advocate. God suffered and endured the most profound abandonment in order to grant us a place to go with our sufferings. In that process the bright light of hope—of resurrection—shines upon our cross and his own, beckoning us to grieve unto life. He is faithful.

STEPS TO HEALING

There are several steps we can take in allowing Jesus to bear our wounding.

First, we must take the time to acknowledge our wounding. This will be difficult for those in the just-get-over-it school of pain management. But our freedom depends on our facing our heart's true response to the incident at hand, be it in the distant past or the recent past. We must make known our suffering. This is not to demonize anyone but rather to confess our response.

The apostle Paul sought to make his suffering known to the Corinthians. He confessed to the church his wounding—a battering ram of nearly intolerable pressures that became for him a sentence of death (2 Cor 1:8-11). We can do the same.

Second, we must seek out safe people who can help bear our burdens. We need the body of Christ for our wounding as surely as we need her for confession of sin. Sin makes us sick, be it our own or another's sin. While no one would claim the church is perfect, we can find healing as we involve ourselves with trustworthy fellow believers.

Third, we must feel freely. Paul confessed despair in his affliction. We, likewise, may need to admit dark and heavy emotions that accompany our suffering. While many of us find it difficult to acknowledge our anger and sorrow, God in his mercy frees us to mourn and to rage. He invites us to identify our wounding with that of Christ.

Jesus confessed to his disciples that his soul was "overwhelmed with sorrow to the point of death." He then invited them to "stay here and keep watch" with him (Mt 26:38). In our times of suffering, Jesus invites us to keep watch with him.

He asks us to do so in light of his resurrection. We identify with Christ in his suffering and in his rising. Paul wanted both—the fellowship of his sufferings and the power of his resurrection (Phil 3:10). So must we seek life amid suffering. The cross of the risen Christ offers us both: death unto life.

Without the hope of resurrection our suffering can readily digress into what Paul referred to as the "worldly sorrow [that] brings death" (2 Cor 7:10). Such sorrow involves a view of suffering as perpetual and unending. From that bleak perspective, the desert contains no oasis, the dark night has no dawn, the cruel cross never gives way to life. Emotion here becomes diseased. Grief is cyclical, and life is veiled in gray and melancholic hues. This is not redemptive suffering.

God wills for our sorrows to give rise to the light of hope. The brokenness we face due to another's sin can in his hands become more ground for his sovereign purpose in our lives. We must grieve at the cross in full view of the empty tomb. Our Good Fridays end rightfully at Easter.

And so, third, some of us may need to take authority over that worldly sorrow that brings death. That means refusing the invitation of hopelessness. Such darkness may take the form of suicidal thoughts, unrelenting sadness or a profound passivity. With the help of others, we can forsake that spirit of death and choose life (Deut 30:19-20). We can suffer actively by taking hold of the promise of release even as we learn to bear pain over a period of time.

Again, we can let Paul guide us here. He saw holy purpose in suffering—the God of resurrection permitted Paul's distress in order to raise him up from it (2 Cor 1:9-10).

Last, we need to exercise the power of resurrection by forgiving our wounders. This is crucial. In order for Jesus to bear our suffering, we must release our captors to him. Our sufferings are bound up into the wounds of Christ when we entrust our perpetrators to him. When we refuse to forgive, we continue to bear suffering without his release. This is a process, which often involves many choices to forgive. But forgive we must, for Jesus' sake and on behalf of our own freedom.

Sufferers who go the way of the cross in their wounds become healers. Annette and Julie both embody a compassion and willingness to suffer long with the wounded. Through their wounds, they know Jesus better. Out of his consolation flows a powerful river of healing from both women. Annette has said that her abuse was a door through which she discovered a more profound revelation of the cross. Her healing has clarified to her who the Messenger is and what her life's message is.

"By his wounds we are healed" (Is 53:5). How profound the sickness of sin is and how deeply it impacts our freedom to become good gifts for others! God has made a way for our restoration. Through the cross we have a place to go with our wounds: death unto life. The result? A greater freedom to love, empowered by intimate reliance upon the suffering and risen Christ. Like Paul, we discover that the very wounds that could have destroyed us become in God's hands an opportunity for joy. Thus the apostle extolled the weakness of his wounds. "That is why, for Christ's sake, I delight in weaknesses, in insults, in hardships, in persecutions, in difficulties. For when I am weak, then I am strong" (2 Cor 12:10).

7

MEN AT THE CROSS

I'll admit it: I'm weak. Much as I would like to begin a chapter on manhood with tales of courage and valor, I can't. Not authentically anyway. The cross has taught me that real power begins with a confession of weakness.

This has special relevance for us as men. Culturally, we are taught that manhood is strength—impassive, initiating power that drives companies and churches, wins battles and woos women with purity and persistence. I love the idea, but I am doomed to fail unless I realize that the threshold over which such virtues are realized is that of weakness. The Father responds to the man who cries out for mercy. That man, in his admitted inability to keep his promises, discovers the greater power of God. That is the beginning and the end of Christ-centered manhood.

How vital this empowering is! The reason I have placed this chapter before the one on the restoration of women is because men's empowering helps make a way for the healing of women. As the gender created first, men have a special responsibility to initiate with women and to serve them.

Don't get me wrong. Jesus is the primary source of both men's and women's security. But man impacts woman profoundly with his sound presence or lack thereof. Thus man's empowering in Christ may set in motion her empowering in Christ. At the same time, the godly empowering of a man renders him increasingly trustworthy, thus granting the woman in his life an invitation to trust him as a part of her security.

OUR NEED FOR HOLY POWER

We as men need holy power. And we have plenty of reasons to cry out for it—for our families, for our sobriety and sanity, for our integrity, for our churches and culture, for the God whose name we bear. He comes quickly to help us. The very weakness that threatens to separate us from him becomes in his hands a mighty source of power. Not only does that power inhibit sin and shame and wounding from taking hold in our weakness, but also he magnifies his power through our very confession of weakness. In so doing, he sets captives free.

Expect warfare before victory. And learn to laugh about it. John Wimber asked me to teach at one of his large international conferences on empowered masculinity. In preparing the message I was harassed relentlessly. I felt unusual homosexual temptations. I felt sick, like I was getting the flu. Then the day before I taught, a woman came up to me, saying she had heard me speak elsewhere a few months before. She claimed that on the previous occasion my broken manhood had been so apparent that she could barely look at me. Gratefully, she added, "You now seem a bit better." Another gift from Christ's body enthusiastically announced to me that I reminded him of his gay psychotic uncle in Australia.

As a result of all this, my thoughts felt clouded and disordered. All that seemed clear was a picture God had given me of a group of men standing before the cross, raising their swords and taking authority over hindrances to their authority as men. But I was afraid. Would I make any sense? Did I possess any real authority, given my weakness and the many reminders of it?

I appreciate the holy place Larry Crabb grants fear when we step out in acts of risky obedience. "A commitment to manly movement *creates* healthy fear. . . . As we resolve to speak in darkness, God gives courage: not the sort that stills trembling legs but the kind that helps us move forward on them."[1] In other words, strength at work in weakness.

Before teaching at that international conference, I cried out for mercy in the presence of brothers and sisters who prayed for me. Then I taught before approximately four thousand people. God honored a simple version of my testimony and aspects of the teaching presented in this chapter. I never felt powerful. But when the men came forward to welcome God's strength in their weakness, the Spirit moved mightily. Clothed with power from on high, we raised the sword of the Spirit over the shaming, wounding and defiling attachments to our manhood. We took an active posture in the Spirit; we cleared away the debris from our humanity. God empowered us in our weakness. We arose in his strength.

Afterward a man came up to me—a big, rough-looking man who seemed angry. *Okay,* I thought. *Why not make it three curses in one conference?* I steeled myself against the feedback to come. But surprisingly his scowl softened and he said, "When you started to teach, I thought, *This is one weak guy—why am I listening to him?* But I watched and I listened. God's power was strong in you. And you know," he whispered, "I need that power too." Strength in weakness. Another reminder of the truth that God chooses the foolish things to shame the wise; he highlights the weak ones of the world to shame the strong (1 Cor 1:27).

CROSS-CENTERED POWER

Striving and jockeying for power are native to fallen masculinity. During a three-day prayer and fasting conference for American male church leaders, I witnessed this tendency in many of the men around me. Even the weakness of fasting did not subdue the competitive drive in some. One successful leader in the Christian men's movement, sporting cowboy duds, came swaggering up to my small group. One of the members introduced him to me and gave a brief description of my ministry, Desert Stream, to him. The guy sized me up and inquired skeptically, "Well, is it big?" Truly it was a locker room moment. I stammered out some awkward answer like "It's big enough."

The way of Christ calls us to die—to turn from the false and worldly ways we have sought to prove ourselves as men, whether it be in the number of churches we have planted or the number of women we have laid, the size of our genitals or our ministries. In that way men who have been ensnared by some pernicious addiction may actually be closer than they know to real manhood. Why? Because they have realized the futility of the world's rewards. They may be ready to surrender all to the King. And when they do, God can raise up in them the version of manhood that pleases him.

But what exactly does God raise up in us? Is it even possible to distill in a few sentences what real manhood is? Any definition, including my own, is incomplete. Still, I will seek to describe what I witness in those men who have died to their fallen attempts at proving themselves worthy.

In essence, those who die to their fallen selves learn to live out of radical dependence upon Jesus Christ. Their lives become centered upon the truth of the One who upholds them in love and trains them in righteousness. Men become true through truthful reliance upon the One. Period. No pretense, no posturing. Just radical commitment to the only One worth dying for.

When such commitment gets worked out in real discipleship and teaching, these men become founded upon the truth in the core areas of their lives. This begins with their sexuality and relationships. When God gets us there, he can lay a sure foundation that will endure until we see him face to face. We can thus approach life out of a truthful base. He lays that base in our lives as we seek to work out our salvation honestly, in the light of God and others, informed by the truth of Scripture.

We expose our sin and he forgives it. We learn to live humble and open lives. He releases us from historic shame that has hovered over our fallen attempts at manhood. We walk uprightly in his honor and refuse the lie that we are less than others. He heals our wounds, which frees us all the more to be reconciled to the good of our manhood.

And we arise in holy power, committed to the truth that has set us free and committed to impart that truth to those around us.

Such men become fit in Christ. Sensitized to the lies of the enemy and their own propensity to deception, true men discern and refuse falsehood. They revere truth. The truth of Jesus Christ has not only made their lives better, it rescued their lives from death. Thus they do not settle for lies—for the false peace common in crossless spirituality these days.

It reminds me of a propaganda poster that the Nazi-run Vichy government in France created during Germany's occupation of that nation in World War II. A husband and wife were looking over a lush field. At their heels were little foxes—one labeled Judaism, the other Churchill, still another de Gaulle. The message was clear: preserve your life by submitting to the powerful ones. Go with the flow; resist the enemies of Hitler and you will live protected, prosperous lives.

Real men cleave to the truth and refuse the little foxes that have the power to destroy soul and body in hell. Like the French resistance fighters who inspired many to refuse the Nazi presence in France, real men resist the lies of this world and implore others to do the same. They then impart Jesus' grace and truth, urging them to arise and resist the cultural tide of sexual immorality and perversion. Their offering is clear: discover holy power in weakness, not the false empowerment of idols.

POWERFUL IN THE TRUTH

The first beneficiaries of a man's empowerment should be those he loves most: his family and friends. A man raised up by Christ is not content to prove himself on the work front to the exclusion of his private life. Truth begins at home. And then God honors a sure domestic foundation by expanding its integrity outward.

For too long we have witnessed the lives of committed saints whose public advances faltered due to a lack of truth behind the scenes. True men know better. Integrity matters, before one or a thousand.

Beyond home, men made true by Christ can leave a rich deposit in their churches and in their greater communities. These who were outcasts, liabilities in the eyes of some, are now pillars in their locales. How? They surrendered. Not in a dramatic, addictive moment but over time, facing their brokenness and the transforming power of Jesus Christ in their weakness. He raised them as they chose (and still choose) to humble themselves before God and one another. At the cross Jesus establishes a level playing field where men together in their brokenness discover the resurrection power of Jesus.

It never ceases to amaze me how Jesus levels us. During one meeting I attended, several of the men in my small group were facing homosexual struggles. At the last minute, a huge, strapping man marched into our group wearing military garb. It seems that the court had ordered him to come to such a group due to his recent arrest for spousal abuse. The other men looked terrified. I could almost hear their teeth chattering as this symbol of all things male (and abusive) barked his confession. I coaxed him to share more.

Underneath the macho exterior was a wounded man. He shared of his experiences growing up on a ranch. When he was ten, his father dropped him off at a house of prostitution and commanded him to go in and prove himself. That set in motion a series of abusive sexual relationships with women, including several relatives. He left home early and went into the military, where his angry view of women as objects to be conquered went unchallenged. But when he described the pain he had inflicted on his wife, he broke down and wept.

The group opened up to him. A couple of the guys shared about their sexual abuse. We prayed for him. Then he looked at the guys and said, "You probably thought I was tough, some kind of real guy. The truth is, we are all broken. We just play it out in different ways." It was a holy moment.

No matter what our affliction is, the cross establishes a level playing field, the humble ground of brokenness on which we can each discover real power. Strength in weakness.

POWERFUL THROUGH RELATIONSHIPS

Weak men become powerful through relationships. We discover early on that we cannot make it on our own. We need God and we need our brothers. To be whole as men, we need the powerful affirmation of other men. This will precede our capacity to fulfill God's call on our lives to love and honor women.

Men are empowered to love women by the Father and his sons. That flies in the face of cultural wisdom that equates manhood with rugged individualism. God has a different way—the humble way of gathering in brokenness, admitting our failures to stay pure and true to our most basic commitments in life. God meets us there and raises up a new breed of men who can love out of his greater power.

So real manhood requires connection with the Father and with one another. Such connection breaks the curse of aloneness that men have faced since the Fall. The truth is, sin inspired in us men a tendency toward isolation and individualism that seems natural to us. That cursed striving undercuts our relationships. But it can be broken through the cross and the church, the fellowship of sinners becoming saints.

Let me remind you of sin's consequences upon men in Genesis 3. Our greater call and commitment to work the ground (from which we were created) turns on us. We now live "through painful toil" (v. 17) and "by the sweat of [our] brow" (v. 19). Our capacity to act and to do digresses readily into a futile activism. Our sense of personal significance rests upon our productivity. This drives us impurely and addictively. It creates fear of real disclosure and reliance upon others. People become the means to our ends. Instead of our greater strength imparting truth and holy order on the earth, that strength drives us back into the earth. Our quest for immortality fails. The end of our striving is death, "for dust you are and to dust you will return" (v. 19).

Such striving isolates us. It blurs our ability to recognize the impact of our brokenness on others and even to recognize our own needs for connection and empowerment. This creates a kind of heartless quality in many men. We become desensitized in our relationships, unaware

144

of our hearts and those around us and thus unable to express our real needs to love and to be loved. We run the risk of becoming relational vagrants—homeless within and thus bereft of a place out of which we can commune with God and others. This generates hostility in our relationships, especially with the women who need us and whose frustration grows as our isolation does.

STRIFE AND SILENCE

We men do not know how to break out of the prison of our solitary striving. We are alone. We feel like we are failing those we love most. Loneliness loves the company of compulsion. Simply add any combination of addictions—chemical, sexual, whatever. The pleasure devolves into shame and contempt, further barring us from real love.

Besides losing our heart, we lose our voices. This can be true in our relationships with men and women, but perhaps especially with women. God called Adam to "rule over" the woman as a consequence for her disobedience (Gen 3:16), yet in spite of that call, men ever since have usually lost verbal battles with women. This may be in part a cultural variable or even a biological one, but it began with the Fall. Even under the best of circumstances, in paradise, the man failed to speak into the darkness of Eve's temptation and sin. The original man was guilty of silence, and so often are we as men.

This is the premise of Larry Crabb's excellent book *The Silence of Adam*. The snake beguiled Eve, but Adam complied with her disobedience. He said nothing to stop her, nor did he refuse her offering of the forbidden fruit. He thus failed her and himself. (And the whole human race, for that matter.) In the Genesis account of the pair's Fall, Crabb sees a picture of our failure as men. "Since Adam every man has had a natural inclination to remain silent when he should speak. . . . Men are uniquely called to remember what God has said and to speak accordingly, to move into dangerous uncertainty with a confidence and wisdom that comes from listening to God. Instead, like Adam, we forget God and remain silent."[2]

145

We forget that God called us to relate freely with himself and others. We were created to know God and then to praise him with our voices for the good gifts he has given to us in our fellow humanity. Our hearts and voices, when joined with others, free us from our aloneness. But sin silences us; it renders us isolated and ashamed, striving alone for an elusive reward.

I believe within most men lies an ancient, deep well of grief and regret. It rumbles with the ache of unexpressed suffering. And in our silence and isolation, the pain fuels our striving and addiction. We thus live in the darkness of unexpressed affliction. Rather than driving us toward relationships, the pain drives us back onto the wheel of striving.

Even the expressed pain of those we have wounded may fail to rouse us to godly repentance. I recall a conference I attended in which women were granted an opportunity to express their pain over how men had dishonored them. A geyser of sobs and screams erupted as those abused and abandoned by men lamented before the cross. Meanwhile I watched the men in the room. They shrunk lower and lower in their seats, descending into an ungodly shame.

Empowered men assume rightful responsibility for the wrong they have done; the silent and disempowered shrink back, reentering the dark waters of grief and regret over their failed attempts at manhood. More unexpressed suffering, more fuel for addiction.

SILENCE OF FATHERS

When I speak of an ancient well of suffering, I refer to our inheritance from preceding generations. And for most of us, that inheritance involved the lack of adequate fathering. I firmly believe that the isolation and silence imprinted on our souls as fallen men is rooted in the fatherlessness native to the Fall. The cycle of sin perpetuates itself father to son. Men who grew up isolated and silent, longing for and yet rarely hearing the empowering voice of the father, often pass down that silence to their sons. Sons who grow up untouched may find it difficult to engage meaningfully with their kids. We inherit and pass on the silence as victims and perpetrators.

So the silence of Adam visits us through a lack of adequate fathering. Such a lack of fathering is common. Though the Father intended for us to be roused and sharpened by our fathers, we find more often than not that our fathers were silent and distant, more shadow than substance in our lives. How blessed are those whose fathers boldly and persistently called their sons into manhood! Still, most of us turn away from our mother's arms into a void. Thus we see how gender security is actually tougher for boys to realize than for girls, since when families falter, it is typically Mother who takes care of the kids. This leaves boys without the masculine voice and presence necessary to discover the solid ground of their manhood.

My father grew up fatherless. He had a wonderful mother who early on divorced her alcoholic husband. She had to become breadwinner and nurturer for her kids. My dad's brother died when he was young, leaving him as the only man in the family. So my dad seemed to grow up alone. As a father in his own right, he did a great job engaging with us as best he could; he sought to love us with honor and dignity. But that fundamental aloneness never left him. And I see that tendency in my brothers and myself, a heightened tendency toward self-reliance, toward going it alone.

A RANGE OF BROKENNESS

Men express their aloneness and silence differently. Some of this depends on personality and on the timing and degree of wounding in relation to their fathers. Some get off the track toward mature manhood earlier than others. This inevitably involves a lack of strong male presence. But it also involves the complex mechanisms of the young heart. We distance ourselves; we drop out of the game when we perceive that the journey toward manhood is too tough and humiliating.

Those who drop out in early childhood may be more vulnerable to deeper problems in their sexual identities, like homosexuality. Same-sex yearnings in a man signal his disidentification with his own masculinity. So he identifies that strength in another and yearns for it sexually. Yet to remain split off from the good of our own power as men is to remain immature.

Others cross the bridge toward identification with the masculine but do so weakly. As children, they make peace with being boys but have yet to emerge into mature and defined manhood. Often these become "good boys," compliant creatures who change colors according to the context, becoming what others expect of them. These chameleons can be defined by the following characteristics: people pleasing, fear of rejection, a fear of being wrong, a tendency toward keeping all options open and not having clearly formulated beliefs.[3] These men are not forces to be reckoned with but timid beings who fear defining themselves. They would rather be nice than truly, powerfully good; they have lost their voices.

Still other men embrace aspects of masculinity—heterosexual prowess, the drive toward competition and power—but do so without a compass or center. Fatherless in their own right, they have managed to identify with the masculine but now compensate for their emptiness by asserting themselves destructively. They target weaker ones, rule heartlessly and seek to win at all costs. They may have much to say, but little of substance. They too lose their voices when it comes to defining and releasing the ache within. Even for the traditional male, that core weakness remains—that essential silence and emptiness, as old as Adam himself.

BREAKING THE SILENCE

Our need for real relationship with God and others remains. I have seen this poignantly in my own father and myself.

My father lost a good friend when his brother-in-law died. During his brother-in-law's funeral, my dad cheerily advanced to the podium to celebrate him. Then unexpectedly he broke down in front of everyone, sobbing over the deceased. In truth my father had lost a friend, one in whom he had put his trust. He did not expect such grief. His heart revealed spontaneously what a rare and valuable gift his friend had been.

We men feel deeply; we simply have a more difficult time expressing the longing and gratitude in our hearts for those who love. Worship leader Andy Park and I became good friends when I transitioned to Vineyard Anaheim in the mid 1990s. We became accountable to each other and poured out our hearts concerning the inevitable trials of advancing the kingdom while tending to our large families.

During a time of painful transition, I remained duty bound; my eyes and feet proceeded onward to face the challenges before me. Time with Andy broke that focused motion. After one prayer session with him, I turned to leave. While I was walking out the door, Andy said to me, "I appreciate your being here." For reasons still not clear to me, I broke down and sobbed. Like father, like son. Andy's encouragement broke the aloneness—his words released living water in the desert of my cursed tendency toward self-reliance.

TRUE IDENTITY AS SONS

We as men need freedom from our cursed emptiness and aloneness. Our release occurs as we discover our true identity as sons of the Father in our fellowship together. As Mike Bickle says, "God wants us to be relationally oriented first and achievement oriented second. . . . We are not first warriors; we are first a bride. We are first lovers, and then we do the acts of war."[4]

Our freedom thus hinges upon two things—an ongoing reliance upon God and a similar reliance upon our brothers. We need look no further than the example of Jesus. He had an enviable childhood, full of the rich feminine love of Mary and the masculine empowerment of Joseph. However, Jesus had to leave home in order to become a man. In spite the wholeness of the holy family, Jesus' manhood hinged upon his entry into the house of his heavenly Father.

Luke 2:48-50 describes Jesus' essential transition. At age twelve he left his parents in order to dialogue with teachers in the temple. Three days later, distraught over his disappearance, his parents found him there. Jesus replied, "Why were you searching for me? Didn't you know I had to be in my Father's house?" (v. 49). Jesus had to shift his identification from his natural family to the Father in order to become a man.

That particular relationship with the Father became the cornerstone of his adult identity. We see this clearly when the Father initiated Jesus' public ministry with these life-defining words: "You are my Son, whom I love; with you I am well pleased" (Lk 3:22).

God graced Jesus with a blessedly whole family of origin. Though many of us cannot say the same, we can follow Jesus' rich example of discovering our manhood in union with the same Father.

We cry out to Jesus in our fatherlessness. He leads us to the Father. That union, along with the progressively clearer identity that results, breaks the curse and its accompanying expressions of loneliness and emptiness. Many of us bear witness to the empty way of life handed down to us by our forefathers. This is not to blame anyone; it is simply to acknowledge that God created us for more than what any family could satisfy. That "more" necessitates becoming responsive to the Father.

Paul wrote:

When we were children, we were in slavery under the basic principles of the world. But when the time had fully come, God sent his Son . . . to redeem those under law, that we might receive the full rights of sons. Because you are sons, God sent the Spirit of his Son into our hearts, the Spirit who calls out *"Abba, Father."* So you are no longer a slave but a son; and since you are a son, God has made you also an heir. (Gal 4:3-7)

The Father breaks through our enslavement to "the basic principles of the world." He does so by establishing us over and over again in the truth that we are his beloved sons. His Spirit displaces our native alienation; he in turn empowers us in our weakness. Instead of relying upon ourselves—our lonely schemes and addictions—we turn to him. We become whole-enough men as the Father actually becomes the center and compass of our lives.

WE NEED OUR BROTHERS

Acknowledging the personal impact of the deadly principles of the world—chemical and sexual addictions, lovelessness in our marriages and families, and so on—to one another is a powerful good. These become the holy ground for discovering with one another the Father's way forward. As we humble ourselves before each other, God deepens in us his liberation. We find our voices as we confess our sin and struggle. We receive and extend his mercy and discover our hearts.

Buried deeply within generations of silence, our hearts begin to express their pain. Like water trickling from an unused pipe, our emotions emerge in fits and starts. But emerge they will. Sons of the good Father discover their hearts and in so doing break ancient strongholds of silence.

Trusted brothers have a unique authority to facilitate this release. Women, in their greater awareness of soul, may encourage such release, but still we need our brothers.

The inadequacy of women's counsel alone is often because the women in our lives may seek to fix our pain. They may also transpose their feminine experience of suffering onto us. Sometimes our pain and struggle wounds them. For example, my confessions to Annette about my pornography addiction wounded her deeply. She needed to know where I was at, but my healing came through my brothers who could stand with me undisturbed.

Yes, we need the objective offering of brothers. Through such fellowship we grow as sons of the one Father and are prepared to love others wholeheartedly.

It is important that we forsake any idealistic notion of finding the lost father of our youth in our male gatherings. Many are looking for that one father figure who will fill in the gaps left by their natural father's inadequacy. If that describes you, look no more! Did not Jesus implore his followers to "not call anyone on earth 'father'" (Mt 23:9)? God alone is worthy of such entitlement. We thus must die to our natural dreams of the perfect human mentor and instead must gather together as brothers to seek and find God.

The cross establishes a level playing field. To be sure, some brothers will be our elders while some will be younger and weaker. Nevertheless, we kneel before the one Father as brothers. There is no man with a greater authority than another to bless his brother. We each possess that call and capacity. The bishop and the busboy stand side by side, imparting the same Spirit of adoption to one another.

Such blessing involves calling forth our brother's true self as a son of the Father. Our word of encouragement toward him empowers him; it may urge him to refuse lesser points of identification. We need this encouragement again and again until we truly believe that we are of the Father. We then, in the power of our sonship, refuse the restless vagrancy of our self-reliance. Each meeting with brothers is a homecoming of sorts in which together we reenter the house of the Father. We need this again and again, like Communion. Our brother represents the sacrament, the witness of Christ revealed through his broken body. In time the living water we extend to each other becomes a more familiar drink than the bittersweet potions of the world.

WORDS THAT EMPOWER AND CHALLENGE

I will never forget the empowering words of a brother I met while living in a Christian men's house at my university. I was young in Christ, still vulnerable to the gay world, yet eager to pursue Christ at all costs. I felt inferior to the other men there. Most were athletic, traditional guys whose life experience seemed light-years away from mine. One man typified this difference yet possessed such a kind and generous disposition that I immediately felt at ease in his presence.

He unexpectedly called me aside one day and simply blessed the

good qualities he saw in me. He expressed gratitude for our brotherhood and for the addition I made to the household. I sailed onto campus that day. A sense of belonging empowered me and displaced any
temptations I may have had to belittle myself. I felt like Peter, who in
all of his compulsions and instability was named a rock by Christ. A
brother had used his power to name me as good and needed. It was
holy power applied to my weakness, like water in the desert.

On the other hand, sometimes the word of a brother is hard—as it
needs to be. For just as we need the sweet substance of encouragement, so we also need the corrective word. Such words pierce the
darkness; they reveal the brokenness that impedes our progress toward
mature sonship. True brothers do not fail to tell the truth. But they do
so in love, in a way that invites us to take a good, hard look at ourselves
in the light of Christ's ever-present invitation to go onward with him.

One brother in the university household challenged my self-reliance. He claimed that I expressed a desire for friendship but still chose
to live alone, bearing another's burdens only when convenient. He
was right. My thick walls incurred loneliness but also gave me the
freedom to live as I wanted, without the restraint of another's needs
and desires. I received his sight in my blindness. I repented and asked
for the grace to become a better friend. That brother challenged some
unused relational muscle. Not only did this improve our friendship; it
also helped prepare me for marriage.

Through our fellowship of brothers God tempers and aligns our
purpose. As mentioned earlier, we as men possess an important need
for significance based upon the work of our hands. We need to be
commissioned to make a difference. In that way healthy brotherhood
must involve a good dose of action. Together, our communion must
possess a forward motion. As each one discovers his place and purpose,
we then rely upon one another to achieve the goal at hand.

Still, one must make an effort to keep service honest through a
willingness to identify and confess the areas in which one is still weak.
We as men were built to be to be outer-directed, piercing the darkness

with truth. But that truth, in order to be pure and merciful, must be established in our private lives. Strength in weakness begins with honest confession among brothers.

So we gather as brothers, seeking power in confessed weakness, while at the same time pointing one another toward higher and truer expressions of our sonship. And no truer purpose exists for us as men than to become those who bless and honor and love women aright. This is crucial to our manhood—without the goal of loving women better, we cease to grow in our manhood. Our honor as men hinges upon our loving the opposite gender honorably. This is because God created us as men to discover his fullness in our communion with women.

WHY WE GATHER AS MEN

Our gathering as brothers is not an end in itself. A community of one gender does not reflect God's highest purposes for humanity. Rather, our meetings are valuable to the degree that they enable us to better honor and serve the women God has placed in our lives. That is among the main reasons why we confess sin together and break the power of our addictions. Why else do we seek to grow in our definition and security as sons and brothers? Why else do we seek to be empowered in our capacity to serve and persevere in love?

These things, of course, involve obedience to the Father. But humanly speaking, we also are motivated by those we seek to love most—the women in our lives. We want to be pure and powerful in our loving initiative toward them, able to give women good gifts as a result of God empowering us in our weaknesses as we gather as brothers. Much of my time in male friendship is spent trying to answer this chief question: how do I better forsake that native self-centeredness and reliance and give to those I love most, especially my wife? Our confessions and prayers bring us that much closer, again and again.

God resurrects holy initiative in men toward the women they love. I see this over and over, particularly with men emerging out of same-sex tendencies, men like Tyler.

A man whose father left the family early on, Tyler was raised by a fine woman but without any masculine authority in the home. His emergence out of homosexuality hinged on his relating to the good masculine power in the men around him. As he received the empowering of brothers, he arose with a new clarity of purpose and definition in his manhood. He experienced a release of desire for women. He is now undaunted in his efforts to discover the one woman with whom he will share his life.

Like Tyler, many men today face an extraordinary need for this empowering. They have often grown up in single-parent homes, typically with the mother in charge of paying the mortgage and making her hard-earned house a home. In short, Mother plays the roles of both parents. Her disappointment and pain toward the men in her life may tempt her to convey to the family her anger, even her disdain, toward the other gender. Her son thus receives a confusing message: men are bad, and I am one!

CONFUSING IMAGES OF WOMEN

The world outside the home can be confusing to a young man as well. Today men grow up in a world of ever-changing gender roles. On the plus side, women have made strides in achieving greater empowerment and visibility in the workplace. That grants women much-needed opportunities to explore the full range of their capacities in the world. But men can readily feel at a loss as to who they are amid such change.

The greater cultural question mark as to what constitutes manhood, when paired with a boy's lack of fathering and the mixed messages he receives about men in his home, can destabilize a young man. This impacts his view of woman. She becomes a larger-than-life presence. He remains small and conflicted toward Mother, needing her support and attention, yet also resenting her for what she cannot be— a father.

His problems with women, often rooted in this close and confusing relationship with Mother, need to be addressed in order for him to be able to love and honor women in his adult life. Tyler, for example, had to face his resentment toward his mother and distance himself from her in order to grow into adulthood. He needed space in order to achieve the goal of truly honoring her. And he had to lay down the judgments, even the hatred he felt toward her for her failures.

It's tough being a mother and a father. And it's equally tough to admit one's antagonism toward the only parent—Mother—who was willing to shoulder the weight. Yet such an admission can be the beginning of freedom for such men—the freedom to love women aright.

A common theme I see in men today is the way they have felt dishonored by the primary women in their lives, beginning with Mother. Wounded women are capable of wounding the men in their lives. Just as women are subject to men dishonoring them, so are men subject to the feminine anger that arises out of such dishonor. Tyler bore the weight of his mother's unhappiness, a grief and resentment rooted in her disappointment with the men in her life.

Many women today are angry at the ways the men in their lives have failed them. And in their wounding, some women arise in unholy power. Such strength functions as a defense against the threat of further hurt. But its function surpasses mere protection. A woman's wounding, if left unattended, can breed contempt and hostility toward the men in her life, including her sons.

WOMEN AS WOUNDERS

During a recent conference, I noticed how a particular female team member was reacting to our host. He was rough hewn yet decent and generous. Still, she winced at nearly every word he spoke. She also slyly undercut him with her cleverness of tongue. Her reaction to the man began to be a problem, hindering our work.

I pulled her aside and invited her to consider her response to this leader. She admitted the difficulty and claimed it was his problem. In truth, however, he was not in error; he was simply being true to how he expressed his masculinity. She admitted that his type of manhood provoked her disdain. I asked her to take a little time out before the Lord and ask him to reveal any hurt or wounding underlying her reaction.

She came back to me later in tears, saying, "That man reminded me of the guys in my life who have let me down." She listed these men, beginning with her father and continuing into the present with several authority figures, including her current employer. She said, "God brought up a whole string of difficult relationships with men in my life. I guess this guy reminded me of them. He brought up a deep wound."

After talking, we prayed and asked for Jesus to bear more of that wound and to grant her the grace to forgive those men who had wounded her. This freed her to accept the leader for who he was. We went on with a renewed freedom to minister together as a team.

When this sort of anger goes undetected, women can employ their verbal prowess to communicate in no uncertain terms that men are less than women and not worthy of their time or trust. When asked recently if she would seriously date a man who was pursuing her, a wounded friend of mine responded wryly, "Nah, I don't need another child in my life." She was a single mother whose husband had failed to support them. Equally sad was the presence of her ten-year-old son, who had heard yet another belittling remark about his gender.

HEALING OF MEN'S DISHONOR

We men often bear dishonor from the women in our lives. It may begin with Mother and continue with girlfriends, wives, colleagues and bosses. Often we do not know what to do with such dishonor. It is unlike wounding from other men. That kind of belittling may be more understandable. We grasp it more readily because it comes from a source closer to our awareness, that is, from the same gender. Often the angry reactions of women toward us puzzle and shame us; they shut down our response because we do not understand the intensity of the feelings. We simply feel guilty for reasons not wholly clear to us. We may have sinned, but why the sustained and powerful reaction?

Prior to an intensive overseas outreach, one of my female coworkers insisted on a conversation before our first meeting. I accepted and she proceeded to rage against me for a loose comic remark I had made a few hours earlier. My foolish quip had displeased her profoundly. She shook with emotion as she described the impact my words had upon her. With great force she insisted that I never address her again in such a manner. She departed abruptly, her boundary-setting mission accomplished.

I felt assaulted. I realized I had sinned with my tongue, but had the punishment fit the crime? The sheer force of her anger left me disempowered and shaken. I could not yell back, let alone push back. The mystery and fire of her wounding wounded me. A few hours later, we spoke again and determined to try and relate better to each other. As it turned out, she had some unspoken, significant conflicts with me. Also, she was in the midst of working out some of the implications of her childhood sexual abuse, including the need to set boundaries with unsafe people. For a fiery season, I had become one of those unsafe people.

Later on I realized that I needed healing from her overreaction to me. I felt as if she had dishonored me with the force of her emotion. The effect on me was twofold. Not only did I want to distance myself from her, but also I wanted to steer clear of any woman who bore similar wounding and the tendency to transfer that anger onto men. I wanted to play it safe. I quietly vowed to not work closely with women who were broken in that way.

But then God nailed me. He revealed not only my hurt but also the defense of dismissing those wounded ones who were earnestly seeking healing yet were still capable of overreacting. I had to admit that in my wounding I could become a rejecter of women.

Tyler faced the same temptation in regard to his mother wounding.

As he sorted out a variety of feelings toward his mother, he realized that he was capable of blessing and cursing her—and not just her but women in general. Though he had no obvious attitude of superiority toward women, he realized that deep in his heart he feared being over-powered and once again rendered small by women in his adult life. This emotional threat prompted him to distance himself from many women, especially strong ones.

Tyler's efforts in sorting out his feelings toward his mother, coupled with the empowering of solid brothers, enabled him to overcome his subtle antagonism toward women.

We as men have an obligation before God to sort out our resistance to the opposite gender. This is true even if our hostility toward women is very quiet. Tyler exemplifies how even a sensitive male is capable of cursing women; that sort of behavior is not the domain of raging tra-ditionalists alone. Thank God for the cross of Christ, through which Jesus put to death our hostility toward women!

We can gather together and allow Jesus to bear the dishonor we have assumed from the women in our lives. He avails himself, Christ crucified, as the One who assumes that hostility and dishonor. Then in his resurrection he empowers us to forgive our feminine offenders. We can stand uprightly and go forward to bless and honor the women in our lives. He frees us to fulfill his purposes for us as lovers of women.

ENTERING THE LAND

We men must accept the risk of engaging with women. I tell the men to whom I minister that the steps they take in this direction may be small, but I urge them to keep taking them. In that process we dis-cover that our fears of the feminine are unfounded. It's an adventure, just like the adventure of scouting out a new land.

Numbers 13—14 describes the Israelites exploring the land of Canaan—a land flowing with milk and honey and laden with much fruit. But with the report of great blessing came also a threat. Some gave a questionable report that the Canaanites were in fact giants, capable of devouring the Israelites, who were reduced to grasshoppers in proportion to the monstrous size of the natives. Fear struck the hearts of the Israelites and caused them to disobey God's call to enter the land and partake of its bounty.

So it is with many of us men. We are not marauders per se; in truth, many of us tend to err on the side of caution. We commit sins of omission—we shrink back in the face of women's power to bless or curse us, to build us up or to dishonor us. As women have discovered their voices and their power, we have lost our own. Rumors of giants tempt us to stay outside of the land, guarded, lonely and safe.

Secure in Christ, we exercise our authority to love. We obey his call to enter the land, facing and forsaking our fears along the way. Blessed are those who do. The Israelites who believed God and not the rumors entered into the land and its richness. Those who grumbled and resisted incurred God's disfavor. They fell in the desert, outside the land of promise.

EMPOWERED TO BLESS WOMEN

The land of promise involves Christ's call for every man to follow his rich example of dignifying women in how he related to them. He honored his female creation freely and without fanfare. His interaction with the Samaritan woman was but one of many demonstrations of how Jesus did this.

Dorothy Sayers wrote of Christ's example, "Perhaps it is no wonder that the women were first at the Cradle and last at the Cross. They had never known a man like this Man—there had never been such another. A prophet and teacher who never nagged at them, never flattered or coaxed or patronised; who never made arch jokes about them, never treated them either as 'The women, God help us!' or 'The ladies, God bless them!' "[5]

Jesus did not pontificate in a politically correct fashion about his high view of women—he simply demonstrated that view in his ministry. His words matched his works. He included women as co-heirs with men of the kingdom reign he initiated. Women served with him and reigned with him in the servant authority he advocated for both genders. John Paul II wrote, "In the eyes of his contemporaries Christ became a promoter of women's true dignity, and of the vocation corresponding to this dignity."[6]

It is Christ who calls us to love women. We who bear his image and likeness must obey the divine command to bless and honor the women in our lives. This is among our chief reasons for gathering as men—to receive the empowering that we need from the Father to arise in love. God's power will meet us at our point of weakness. Instead of shrinking back, remaining safe yet still bound to our aloneness, we will be freed by God to become sources of life for women. Through the cross the Father has made a way for those weakest among us to realize his power in our masculinity. He makes us solid through our brothers, for our women.

Weakness poses no threat to God's purposes in our lives as men. We gather to break out of our aloneness as well as the shame of relational and sexual failures. There we discover the cross, God's power realized in the weakness of the Son. We thus find communal identification with the One who makes us strong. He empowers us, not in spite of our weaknesses, but in them. As brothers together, joined with the One not ashamed to call us his brothers, we grow in our capacity to love well. In so doing we give glory to our Father and extend his rule on earth.

8

WOMEN AT THE CROSS

We live in an age marked by women's advancement in most spheres of life. The "gentler sex" has demonstrated its strength and capability, both inside and outside the home. To highlight woman's weakness may therefore seem unjust and counterproductive to the cause of her full equality with men in the world today. Nevertheless, in this chapter we return to our central theme—how our human weaknesses attract the strength of God.

Paul's boast "When I am weak, then I am strong" (2 Cor 12:10) applies as pointedly to women as to men. Yet a woman's weakness differs from that of a man. Understanding that difference may be key to her welcoming the strength she needs in order to live in freedom before God and others.

In instructing married couples Peter described the wife as "the weaker partner," but he also said that wives are "heirs with [their husbands] of the gracious gift of life" (1 Pet 3:7). So men and women are equal as heirs together, and yet somehow the wife differs from the husband in her weakness. Peter did not explain the nature of the difference, except to urge men to treat their wives with consideration and respect in light of their greater weakness. I believe the special care involves woman's most blessed strength and painful vulnerability—her relational gifts and her corresponding need for security in her relationships.

RELATIONAL STRENGTH AND WEAKNESS

My wife is a powerful woman whose calling to teach and publish and strategize is a mighty one. Yet in introducing herself, she defines herself primarily in terms of her relationships with me and with our children. Her definition and well-being hinge more on the nature of her relationships than on her vocation. Because of the relative degree of health we enjoy in our family, Annette thrives in both arenas.

But not all women discover that secure relational base. I minister to countless women whose eyes convey a hardness and a hopelessness due to the betrayals they have suffered. Wounds of abuse, neglect and abandonment have calcified into embittered, distorted patterns of fulfilling their needs for love. Their strengths have become weaknesses. Their responsive and nurturing hearts, beautifully intended to house the mysteries of love, have become receptacles of profound pain and curdled emotion.

For many women, men are the enemy. The good that God intended for women has become subject to the perils of sin. The Fall's consequences cannot be minimized here—our creative strengths can become weaknesses. But such a deformation can be brought under the authority of Christ Jesus and reversed.

Consider here the difference between men's strength (and potential weakness) and that of women. While men seek to master realities outside of themselves through the works of their hands, women excel at imparting life in communion with others. Nothing exemplifies this truth more than motherhood.

Woman alone is capable of housing another life and then nurturing the newborn. Life begins in the sheltering womb and is advanced in the fusion of being between mother and child. That essentially feminine quality flows freely out of whole-enough women. It distills a woman's "special gift of making herself at home in the inner world of others," to quote Edith Stein.[1]

John Paul II described women as possessing "special communion with the mystery of life."[2] Motherhood enhances that communion through a woman's unique contact with life within herself. This profoundly marks her connection with others in general. The true feminine in a woman grants her the gift of connecting with others—paying attention to them—in a manner that surpasses a man's relational focus.

SPECIAL CONNECTION WITH OTHERS

The relational gift in women is rooted in creation. Whereas Adam was formed from the dust (Gen 2:7), Eve emerged from Adam (v. 22). In other words, she was formed out of a human being, not from an inanimate source. That laid the base for woman's heightened relational sensitivity and gifting. She naturally welcomes communion with others, a quality that issues out of a profound well of wisdom and meaning that she draws from such relating and imparts to her relationships. What a treasure this well holds for all people! Without it, both genders wither. Our capacity to engage meaningfully with others is rooted in the nourishment we have received from women, beginning with our mothers.

Mary, the mother of Christ, exemplifies this amazing capacity to bear life, draw meaning from that emerging life and extend life to others. She welcomed the call to serve God by bearing Christ. Gabriel's announcement that God would overshadow her did not prompt fear so much as a faithful response. "'I am the Lord's servant,' Mary answered. 'May it be to me as you have said'" (Lk 1:38).

We glimpse the depth of her feminine soul as Mary marveled at the Nativity. Upon witnessing the response of the angels and the shepherds, she "treasured up all these things and pondered them in her heart" (Lk 2:19). Hers was an essentially feminine heart, set apart by the Father to glorify and magnify himself. She joined with the Father and bore a life that would perform mighty deeds, scatter the proud, bring down rulers from their thrones and lift up the humble (1:51-52).

Mary represents the power of woman's relational gifting. She receives love, imparts love and bears fruit in such relationships—fruit that remains. In defining the true feminine in woman, John Paul II wrote, "A woman's dignity is closely connected with the love which she receives by the very reason of her femininity; it is likewise connected with the love which she gives in return."[3] I've seen this in my own wife.

During our courtship, Annette and I changed a lot. We pressed through a lot of unknowns, both spiritually and emotionally. For Annette's part, she faced my challenge of her somewhat tepid spirituality. Though a long-standing Christian, she was not yet walking in dynamic personal communion with the Father. I urged her to join with me in attending my church (a charismatic fellowship).

One day she greeted me with a fresh and glowing account of how she had received the outpouring of the Spirit as others had prayed for her. She sounded different. She looked different. Something had softened in her; she shone with an inner light. Her renewed womanhood captivated me. That difference helped ease my fear of emotional intimacy and commitment.

As Annette continued to welcome God into the deep places of her soul, my attraction to her increased. Her emerging womanhood roused all the more my still-awakening manhood. Through Annette, I was coming to grasp Victor Hugo's description of "a softer radiance and a greater mystery, woman."[4]

WOMEN AT RISK

Woman's strong yet exquisite relational capacity—the gift of receiving and giving love—can turn on her. Sin places at risk the good of woman's responsiveness to love. She becomes subject to two enemies of her true femininity: the tendency to overidentify with her human relationships and the misuse of her womanhood by fallen men.

Here one cannot underestimate the power of the Fall upon gender relating. God defined consequences on Adam and Eve for their disobedience, and those consequences turned their strengths into potential threats to their personal and interpersonal wholeness. God said to the woman,

Your desire will be for your husband,
and he will rule over you. (Gen 3:16)

This signaled a change in the relational dynamic between men and women.

Under the Fall, woman tends to rely inordinately upon man to define and guide her. She bends into a fellow creature, man, sometimes making an idol of him. And thus sin scrambles the order. Rather than responding to God first, then welcoming and nurturing the man second, woman gives a created being the upper hand.

The risk here is obvious. As woman bends into man, he can assert an authority that will damage her. He can use his power to dishonor her—to employ her exquisite responsiveness for his own advantage. She yields to him foolishly, and he brutishly turns her strength into a weakness.

When mistreatment by man occurs, woman becomes subject to dishonor, even hatred, of her essential and exquisite offering. This is misogyny, a Greek word meaning "hatred of woman." It is among the most profound consequences of sin upon God's image.

Woman's domination by man seriously obstructs her ability to become a good gift of love for others. Hereditary sinfulness, as expressed in such broken complementarity, breaks down her dignity, the true stature that God assigns her in union with himself. It robs her of her freedom to receive and to give love. And in so doing, it imperils all of us.

Beaten-down women, especially mothers, will often fail to arise in the security and strength that liberates their offering of love to others. But this distortion applies to more than just family life. Such sinfulness finds expression, in the words of John Paul II, "in different spheres of social life: the situations in which the woman remains disadvantaged or discriminated against by the fact of being a woman."[5]

A Depth of Dishonor

Woman's profound soul—that well of wisdom Karl Stern associates with "the veiled and the hidden"[6]—can become a dumping ground for dishonor. Her soul gathers and retains the sins of dishonor. In this respect women differ from men. They possess a deeper bank in which historic offenses are deposited. Collectively, these deposits can become millstones that weigh down and even crush her feminine soul. Thus the fallen counterpart of Mary's pondering the wonder of the Nativity in her heart is wounded women's agonizing over the damage inflicted upon them by men.

A woman bears her wounds deep within. Misogyny becomes imprinted on her soul—a brand that distorts her self-esteem and even her most basic offerings as a woman. For example, Annette bore the dishonor of sexual abuse from her childhood. She internalized the assault profoundly, and it shook the secure foundation of her girlhood. Much of this was unconscious. She struggled with horrific nightmares, anxiety attacks and unexpected bouts of depression. She had received a lot of healing by the time our first son, Gregory, was born. But even then the assault on her womanhood twenty-four years earlier prevented her from breast-feeding him. Something within her had shut down, and in spite of much effort, she could not produce milk.

A woman is more vulnerable than a man to others because she possesses greater sensitivity in her relationships. This can be for better or worse, to receive honor or dishonor. The effect of masculine assault upon her reveals the power of her ability to internalize the devastation. It also reveals woman's greater need for protection from redeemed men.

Paul Quay writes of a woman's heightened need for security in light of her bodily weakness. Her physical vulnerability to assault may produce fear in her. "Without [security], even her physical fertility . . . is further reduced. But when secure, the woman nourishes her child with the milk from her own breasts; and a nursing mother is that which a man must protect above all else."[7]

So a woman needs a certain amount of relational security in order to thrive as a woman. But what if she is already insecure? She can begin by facing her insecurities, including the destabilizing effects of misogyny. Then she can begin to receive the healing that Christ and his body has for her. Such healing can allow love to be established within her, providing the security she needs. The power of his love, becoming mature in her weakness, lays a solid base for relating.

TYPES OF MISOGYNY

What are the various expressions of misogyny? Among the most destructive is the sexual abuse and assault of women. As we have seen, the misuse of male sexual power (this includes childhood sexual abuse, rape and all manner of sexual harassment) preys upon woman at her most vulnerable point. God intended her sexuality to be the site of fruitfulness; there her choice-making faculty is crucial in welcoming only those worthy of her trust and honor.

Hugo wrote of the holy ground of emerging feminine sexuality, "Woman in the bud is sacred. . . . The possibility of touch should increase respect."[8] And so sexual assault violates what is sacred. It engenders fear and dread within a woman. The masculine assault of females desecrates holy ground, perverting the site of new life into one of shame and despair.

Second Samuel 13:1-21 illustrates poignantly the devaluation of women through sexual assault. Amnon tricked his sister into tending to him while he lay in bed. He then raped her, as he was stronger than she. Upon consummating the act of violence, he then "hated her more than he had loved her" (v. 15). Amnon said to Tamar, "Get up and get out!" After the rush of his release, she became only a reminder of his sin and shame. Amnon defended himself against his evil by banishing the object of that evil.

Tamar resisted banishment on the grounds that such disfavor would only add insult to the injury she had sustained (vs. 16-17). But Amnon's power prevailed. She was cast off, left to live the rest of her life as "a desolate woman" (v. 20). We might assume that she never received an adequate response to her cry, one she made while seeking to fend off her rapist: "Where could I get rid of my disgrace?" (v. 13).

The disgrace engendered by sexual assault is but one expression of misogyny. It differs from others in that it is readily identifiable. Most misogyny is subtle; sins of dishonor against women often express themselves in sly sins of omission or commission that convey the belief that women are less than men. The theme of masculine superiority pervades some quarters, even Christian ones.

For example, Annette once worked on a church staff governed by a strong "boy's club" mentality. The male "players" (everyone on the staff except Annette) sought the favor of the head "coach" (the pastor) continuously. Once, during a strategy meeting, Annette had an idea that could save a lot of money and time on a given project. The head coach being absent on the occasion, one male associate volunteered to run her idea by the senior leader. During a coffee break, Annette overheard that particularly ambitious pastor pitching her idea to the boss as if it were his own. He received much honor for it. "I guess only men qualify as keen thinkers here," she later confessed.

Annette was amused by the incident. She knew her ideas had merit, and frankly she found her associate pathetic in his duplicity. Some women, however, do not believe their thoughts and feelings matter as much as men's do. Inevitably these women were socialized in environments where misogyny was a governing family rule.

Kay grew up watching her father abuse her mother. Most of his violent words and behaviors were aimed at what he perceived to be female weakness and incompetence. He dissuaded Kay from using her mind, trying instead to make her want to be a compliant homemaker.

Kay's father was also a misogynist in his sexual unfaithfulness to her mother. When men promise to uphold their commitments to women—financially, emotionally, sexually—then break their promises, women's legitimate need for security is undermined. This injures the fragile beauty of womanhood; it breaks trust and tempts a woman to hide and harden her native responsiveness to the man in her life. She often must get bigger, larger than life, to cope with the absence of love and practical support.

How many women today have had to face infidelity via a man's addiction to pornography? Men who are sexual addicts may be oblivious to the impact of their sin upon others, but to women it is nothing short of infidelity. And again, infidelity is misogyny—an expression of dishonoring women. Through the computer, men invite other lovers into the bedroom. At that site of trust and intimacy, male addicts betray their real female partners. Many women naturally close off their hearts to them. This can contribute as well to women's own misogyny—a hatred of themselves for not being appealing enough to compete with virtual partners.

Misogyny is passed down from one woman to another; it is not only transmitted man to woman. Kay's mother believed her husband when he screamed at her for not doing the dishes right, ridiculed her opinion or took on a new mistress. *He's right,* she thought. *I am stupid and undesirable; I deserve no better.* In agreeing with the lie and complying with the dishonor, the mother encouraged the misogyny of her daughter.

Annette and I are continually amazed at how women are often less encouraging than men of other women when they step into nontraditional challenges, like church leadership roles. The loudest naysayers we have known are unbelieving women. It is as if they project their own insecurities onto their sisters, assigning them evil or at least neurotic motivations. Like a radioactive baton in a relay race, destructive misogyny gets passed on again and again.

THE CURE FOR MISOGYNY

The cross is the one place where misogyny can find its end. Regardless of its expression—be it abuse, abandonment or a woman's self-hatred—Jesus died to bear the sin of misogyny. The crucified One answers the laments of the Tamars everywhere as they cry out, "Where could I get rid of my disgrace?" One must look no further than the place of great exchange—the cross, where God bears disgrace and grants women holy honor instead.

The church of Jesus Christ then reveals the power of that cross-centered victory upon the earth. His body must seek to ensure that such liberation prevails over all manner of dishonor and division between men and women. The church is Christ's home on earth where those oppressed by misogyny can be set free. The bride alone, in union with him, possesses the authority against which hell's power will not prevail (Mt 16:18). This includes authority over the strongholds of misogyny.

We gather as the broken bride and confess the stronghold of this unique strain of sin-sickness. There is power in acknowledging the damage done and even recognizing that some women believe they have deserved the damage inflicted on them by broken men. At times I have been nearly unable to teach on the subject as a result of the corporate pain and rage in the gathering. Only tears can express the Father's heart for those betrayed in the most vulnerable parts of their feminine hearts and bodies. But with the tears must also come the clear word of recognition—"This happened to me and it was profoundly dishonoring." Then, with its confession, Jesus can bear the unbearable weight of the particular strain of misogyny.

As in the healing of all our wounds, the beginning of that healing occurs with the naming of one's wound and the placing of it into Christ's wounds. The wound of misogyny is no exception. But of course a woman's identification with the crucified One in his suffering will often have much emotion attached to it. Women may need a lot of space and opportunity to release the depths of pain associated with misogyny.

In particular I have met people of certain ethnic groups in which women have historically been so devalued that they were often destroyed at birth due to not being boys. Even though such extremities of evil may not be operative in the lives of those to whom we minister, the shadow of dishonor, even death, may still rest on them. We want to give the Holy Spirit an opportunity to reveal the impact of misogyny, in whatever forms it may take. Then we give the Lord of each soul opportunity to reveal the unique strain of misogyny, to release the corresponding pain and finally to bear its weight at the foot of his cross.

FREEDOM FROM SELF-HATRED

Women may need to identify the ways they have agreed with their accusers. As we have already noted, women will often concur with the misogynists in their lives. They will internalize the lies of inferiority and dishonor. Again, the witness of the Spirit at work in the women is crucial. A woman must answer the question "To what degree have I complied with my abusers and accusers?" She may need to confess that she has become a misogynist in response to the misogyny in her life.

A corresponding confession involves that of hating oneself as a woman. This involves the subtle perception that one deserves no better than abuse or abandonment. This perception can be empowered by an equally subtle belief that men actually are better than women. Where a woman views men as having all the power, and therefore concludes that the male is the superior gender, she needs to name and confess this belief as her own sin.

The sword of dishonor from another can become a sword of division within a woman's soul, separating her from her own honor as a woman. But as she confesses her own misogyny, Jesus removes a significant barrier to her freedom. He heals the divide in her soul, thereby freeing her for holy acceptance of her gender and personhood.

The depth and intensity of the process of Jesus bearing misogyny can be understood in light of the depth of the feminine soul. I have already addressed the large well that women possess—a container that bears honor and dishonor. Those who suffer misogyny for years will possess quite a storehouse of suffering. For some, that deep well will be the source of contempt—deep roots of hatred for men.

FACING MISANDRY

Women who have been profoundly wounded by men will often exhibit a lot of misandry. In other words, self-hatred is not the only feminine response to misogyny; some women will conceive hatred toward their offenders. This contempt gives rise to thick walls of bitterness and self-protection toward the men who have dishonored them.

It is right to recognize sins against oneself and to refuse them as one's destiny. However, once a woman has recognized these sins, she has a choice: to forgive her offender or not. The consequences of not forgiving are profound. First, as Jesus says, the Father will not forgive us if we refuse to free our captors by forgiving them (Mt 6:14-15).

Second, a woman's embittered response to the one or several men who dishonored her can readily become generalized onto all men. Unforgiveness can contribute to a distorted lens that blurs her capacity to perceive accurately half the population. That prevents her from fulfilling Christ's law of love. It also undercuts who she is as one created to bear God's image in harmony with the opposite gender.

Third, unforgiveness fuels a kind of self-defensiveness—the boast that one's rage is one's pride and power. That kind of justice, popular in secular "survivor" groups today, actually empowers a distinctly non-Christian strain in a woman. It masculinizes her. Rather than the Father empowering her in weakness, such "justice" empowers the false self. Such a woman is unable to accept her inspired feminine sensitivity as well as her appropriate need for men.

This type of self-defensiveness is on the increase in our world today. As a result, more and more wounded women, empowered by the injustices they bear, can barely tolerate men. Some are forsaking their need for them altogether.

JUSTICE AND HEALING

John Paul II has called women to not become like men in their anger and so suppress their real womanhood. Justice must not "lead to the masculinization of woman," he said, for when it does, women "deform and lose what constitutes their essential richness."[9] I have seen that "essential richness" hang in the balance for many fine women. God revealed a depth of suffering related to misogyny in them, and he called each to draw upon his grace, deeper still, to forgive their captors.

One colleague of mine said this: "I had to choose—either the way of the cross or radical feminism." Gratefully, she chose the cross. In so doing, she participated in her healing by releasing the particular sources of dishonor that had wounded her. That in turn freed her from some of her defenses. (Their removal is a process as one learns to trust God and others from the heart.) Her willingness to forgive also granted God and others that much more room to pour in the honor and holy power for which she longed.

One key is the power of representational forgiveness. Here men who have repented of their own misogyny will represent their gender in seeking the forgiveness of wounded women. One who has been an unfaithful husband may confess and repent on behalf of other adulterous husbands. Other men may represent absentee fathers, abusers or cruel brothers and boyfriends. We have done this now for years in our Desert Stream groups and conferences. Each time we do, God releases women's hearts with his mercy. Their actual offenders may never repent, yet as these women witness men honestly repenting of misogyny, God releases grace in their hearts to forgive their offenders.

Another key is discovering in community men who are safe and yet strong in the Lord. At first women emerging out of misogyny will view these men with suspicion, but once their fears go unrealized, these women can slowly come to value the contribution of men, even to their own lives. In that respect these men truly represent repentant males, not only in a prayerful confession but in the witness of their lives. This too will quicken the process of women forgiving their offenders.

RENUNCIATION WITH JUSTICE

Two other pieces of advice may lend strength and objectivity to the woman whose life has been marked by misogyny.

First, I suggest that she not only confess misogyny but also renounce it. By that I mean she should reject, in Jesus' name, the spiritual and psychological strongholds that underlie the inferiority she

174

feels. In some cases, I believe, the enemy of our souls actually empowers those thoughts. He harasses helpless ones with this theme of dishonor.

I saw an example of this in the life of a colleague of mine who had been sexually assaulted throughout her childhood and who, even in adulthood, encountered men who would harass her. We prayed for her. Then a friend sensed a word from God about demonic harassment in the case. My colleague prayerfully rejected that demonic source of misogyny, and then, with our support, she exercised her own spiritual authority over that lifelong theme.

Something dark lifted from her. Our ministry to her not only cleared the air of a lot of the public harassment she had faced (most of it stopped); it also empowered her to become a "misogyny-free zone," one on whom belittling words and temptations could not land. Renouncing misogyny empowered her to stand and to learn to walk in the world without being subject to its misogyny.

Another piece of advice is to avoid becoming overzealous in identifying misogyny. What I mean is that for some persons nearly everyone seems to be a misogynist. They are suspicious about men and women alike who do not grant every woman the highest possible place. These people need to learn how to discriminate between objective expressions of dishonor and a difference of opinion.

For example, a woman came to me lamenting over her misogynistic pastor. When asked about the specifics of his dishonor of women, she spoke of how he did not believe that women should be senior pastors. She also mentioned her disappointment in not being asked to preach more often in the church. (An excellent teacher, she preached in the church approximately once a year.) When I asked her further about his approach to women, she admitted that he was inclusive and embracing of them. In fact, she was one of the elders of the church. I helped her to see that she and her pastor possibly had a difference of opinion over how to interpret the Scripture in regards to women and senior leadership. I also urged her to try to distinguish between disappointment and dishonor.

Many women will tend to transfer blame for pain from their past onto men in the present. In reality, though, however imperfect these men are, many of them are not actually guilty of the sins of their predecessors. Wise, trustworthy counselors can help determine that difference for wounded women in the healing process. Such guides need to be as objective as they are supportive. Justice is at stake here. Just as a woman emerging out of misogyny does not want to come back under dishonor, so she should be equally intent on not dishonoring others through misplaced judgments.

UNFAILING ADVOCACY

At the center of freedom from misogyny is woman's unfailing advocate—Jesus Christ. He is her defender from the world's harassment, the silencer of any demonic accusation, the greater power in her weakness. In seeking him, and her cure at his cross, she has full access to the strength that secures her in love. And that security is crucial to her well-being as a woman.

Jesus must become that greater source of security in the lives of women. Why? Because in light of the fallen world in which we live, a woman cannot successfully make a created being her security. As we have seen, this is among a woman's greatest temptations. Created from man, she may tend to rely inordinately upon a man for her well-being. A futile quest! No human being can make us well.

Only the Creator can love us unfailingly. Those emerging out of the power of misogyny (and their own wounded reactions to it) have a rich opportunity to grasp that truth. These women know their need to emerge out of their bent positions and to arise, at last upright in the hope of Christ. God often waits until we recognize that our idols cannot save us; he then gently invites us into deeper communion with himself—the only One who can save us.

Out of that yielded posture, a woman can then receive the healing that Jesus wants to give her. This is nothing less than the restoration of her true feminine response to him as well as to trustworthy others. Helpful here are supportive women who understand her wound and its cure. Equally helpful are sensitive yet strong men who grant women a new view of what men can be—empowering and respectful. The healing a woman receives from others will free her to love people all the more. But the source of that healing is clear—this is Christ who is setting her free to be a woman. His "priests" will come and go. Jesus alone, working through a variety of individuals and groups, is the Liberator.

The Gospels are absolutely clear on the saving work of Christ among women—his unfailing love in restoring their dignity though his communion with them. John Paul II noted "a resonance of heart and mind" between Christ and the women in the New Testament. "Jesus expresses appreciation and admiration for [their] distinctly 'feminine' response" to him.[10] From the beginning of his life on earth to its end, women played key roles in devoted service to him. They demonstrated a special sensitivity to him that was characteristic of their femininity.

Out of this profound response of heart to him, they emerged as powerful disciples. In fact, they appear to have surpassed the male disciples in their strength of commitment to him. All the male disciples fled at his crucifixion. It was "women [who] were in the forefront at the foot of the cross. . . . In this most arduous test of faith and fidelity the women proved stronger than the apostles."[11]

Christ empowers women to know him and to arise in the honor that only their Creator can grant. A woman's very weakness—that heightened need for security in relationships—can become a source of profound power. That power issues out of ever-deepening communion with him. And in that process God will reveal the barriers to receiving that honor.

The Lord demonstrated this to the Samaritan woman. Christ said to her, "If you knew the gift of God . . . " (Jn 4:10). He then invited her to partake of the living water—a heavenly stream that would satisfy her soul and secure her in love forever. Similarly he invites every woman to receive that gift. He bears the dishonor of misogyny in his suffering. And in his resurrection he pours unfailing love and honor into woman's depths.

Strength in weakness. Rather than despise her need for relationship, a woman can rejoice in the One who beholds her need for love and seeks to meet it. In tender communion with God and his community, a woman is restored. God frees her to rejoice in the full range of her inspired humanity this side of heaven. Though not untouched by the world and its perils, she can live in freedom, her very weakness secure in his unfailing love.

9

§

HOMOSEXUALITY AND THE CROSS

In my residual struggle with homosexuality I am reminded again and again of God's strength at work in my weakness. Don't get me wrong. God has done tremendous healing in my life. He bore my shame—I no longer feel bad or unacceptable about my particular weakness. He carried my sin—I no longer conceive thoughts or acts of homosexual sin. And God is faithful to continue to heal areas of wounding in my life that contribute to my vulnerability. But at times that weakness arises. I ache for what can never be mine and for what God can never bless.

And in those temptations I turn to the One who upholds me according to his powerful love. He closes the gap of my loneliness and reminds me that he is enough. Sometimes the love of Annette and trusted friends mediates this sufficiency, but at other times I seek only Jesus. He shines through the window of my weakness. I cling to him and he imparts the love and objectivity I need to stand strong.

As the temptation passes, Christ empowers me once more to love those I hold dearest—my family and my colleagues in healing ministry. These words of Jesus to Peter have special relevance to me in such times: "Simon, Simon, Satan has asked to sift you as wheat. But I have prayed for you, Simon, that your faith may not fail. And when you have turned back, strengthen your brothers" (Lk 22:31-32). He equips me for every good work that he wills—strength in weakness.

And I am able to proceed with fresh compassion. Having been empowered by his grace anew, I can give it away freely.

Meister Eckhart said there are two sorts of people: the one that is constituted with little impulse to do wrong and the one that is strongly tempted. The latter kind of person "is easily swayed by whatever is at hand. . . . He therefore fights hard against whichever vice is most natural to him. . . . These people are more to be praised than the first kind. Their reward is also greater and their virtue of much higher rank. For the perfection of virtue comes of struggle."[1] Divine strength matures in us as we consistently submit our weaknesses to God.

BELOVED PROPHETIC WITNESSES

I am consistently empowered by the witness of men and women around the world who have allowed Jesus to strengthen them in their own homosexual struggle. I think of Markus Hoffman of Germany and Toni Dolfo-Smith of Canada. Both of these men, now paired with wonderful wives, have pioneered numerous expressions of hope and healing for the sexually and relationally broken in their lands. Because of their willingness to welcome God into their homosexual struggles, he has released his power through them. Both have dedicated their lives to transforming the church into a place where others can discover the God who strengthens the weak.

I think of Sue Hunt, an English woman who in her lesbian struggle sought out Buddhist spirituality as a way of making sense of her life. She came to know Christ while in a Buddhist monastery and immediately began to seek and serve the One. Her healing deepened over time and she became a missionary in Thailand. There she has found great favor in a variety of churches, imparting the hope of the God who strengthens the weak, particularly in areas of sexual brokenness.

God called Maria Cardenas out of lesbianism many years ago. She entered into the deep waters of healing and allowed God to lay a sure foundation of strength in her weakness. She now travels throughout the world, particularly in Presbyterian circles, proclaiming and imparting the power of the Lord's transforming love amid her weakness.

I recently traveled with Maria to Argentina. There she shared of her background and of her then-current temptation in a dating relationship. It seems this man wanted to go further sexually than Maria was willing to go. As a result of her resistance, he lost interest and she lost a boyfriend. She wept as she recounted that loss. Her expressed struggle for intimacy and integrity in relationships inspired the entire church.

Perhaps this is because Maria, in her weakness, as well as Sue, Toni and Markus in theirs, all aspire to intimacy and integrity in the light of God's greater power. Their stories, and thousands more like theirs, apply to more than just the homosexually vulnerable. They speak to all who seek Christ amid their brokenness. For in their journeys we behold the faithfulness of Christ—we catch a glimpse of the cross, emblazoned on human hearts. They fulfill Leanne Payne's words: "Truly, to write of the healing of the homosexual is to write of the healing of all men everywhere."[2]

But that healing is contingent upon relying upon the One again and again. He provides the strength to live in freedom with each new experience of weakness. Without doubt, he is able to restore the homosexually vulnerable in an instant, and I believe he sometimes does so. Interestingly, though, God rarely calls these exceptional ones to proclaim and impart freedom to others. Such healing ministry is typically entrusted to those whose healing occurs gradually. The ones who rely upon him daily for the grace, truth and transforming power needed to live in the light—these are the weak ones through whom God's strength is most clearly revealed. Compassion flows out of their suffering and out of their daily gratitude for God's great and deeply personal faithfulness to them. Strength in weakness.

A PROPHETIC ARMY

God is forming a healing army of men and women coming out of homosexuality. This army is a prophetic witness for the church and the world. Through the witness of his strength at work in their weakness, God is revealing who he is—full of grace and truth. And he is revealing who he wants all of us to be—a people desperately dependent upon him.

The writer of Hebrews spoke of an army whose "weakness was turned to strength; and who became powerful in battle and routed foreign armies" (Heb 11:34). But why an army composed of homosexual strugglers? And why such a battle?

Obviously, relational brokenness applies far beyond same-sex tendencies. Those who struggle homosexually are a tiny minority of the population. But nowhere is the battle for truth more evident than in the thick confusion that surrounds homosexuality in the world and in the worldly church today. Many other sexual and relational issues are clearly delineated. Most would believe abuse and addiction, even marital breakups, to be destructive and in need of a cure. Not so with homosexuality. It has become, in the words of Thomas Schmidt, "the battleground for all the forces seeking to give shape to the world" of the new millennium.[3]

Consider these disturbing signposts of the battle for truth surrounding homosexuality. (My references derive mostly from recent events in the United States, but their corollaries can be found in most other Western nations.)

In the early 1990s Bill Clinton declared that homosexuality was the last great battlefield of civil rights in America. Since that time most states have considered, and many have approved, benefits for same-sex partnerships as well as adoption rights for gay couples.

In the media the face of homosexuality has never been more clever, winsome or sexy. Gay characters are now standard in television dramas and situation comedies. In that respect the entertainment industry in Los Angeles has become the center for transforming opinion about homosexuality. From New Jersey to New Delhi, idealized gay men and women are coming out of the closet and into our living rooms. The lack of negative public response to such media portrayals suggests that our minds are changing about homosexuality. What was once novel and disturbing about homosexuality is now deemed acceptable, even enjoyable.

The American Psychiatric Association (APA) recently determined that any kind of therapy aimed at helping gays change is unhealthy and wrong, unethical according to the group's professional standards.[4] The APA's bias against the prospect of change was revealed in their response to a world-class study crafted by one of their associates, Dr. Robert Spitzer.

Spitzer is the neuropsychiatrist who led the charge to remove homosexuality from the books as a psychological disorder in 1972. Much later, though, he explored the possibility of changing one's homosexuality in a study that involved in-depth interviews and follow-up with individuals who claimed to have experienced lasting change.[5] Spitzer, a non-Christian, spent years on this study and released his findings in early 2001. The result was clear: of the two hundred men and women with homosexual backgrounds whom he studied, 66 percent of the men and 44 percent of the women were currently engaged in sustained, loving heterosexual relationships.

The APA dismissed the study as beside the point, and most major newspapers gave it little exposure. Spitzer reeled at the lack of objectivity he observed and the rancor his work provoked. He claimed that he had never experienced that kind of professional prejudice at any other time in his career.

A NEW PREJUDICE

We are facing a new bias in the West today—a bias declaring that anyone who challenges the inherent goodness of homosexuality is morally defective. This bias stems, paradoxically, from the new tolerance—a powerful belief system asserting that all points of view are equally valid simply because one holds to it. Thus, for the active, realized homosexual in today's culture (and for those sympathetic to their position), the goal is for homosexuality to be accepted on a par with heterosexuality. Anyone who challenges that goal is intolerant. The only "sin" in that system is to assess one way of life as better than another.

I recently challenged a group of confused teenagers and their gay adviser at a public high school. They were seeking the right to congregate on the basis of their homosexuality—to confirm themselves and others as gay in a school-sponsored club. We fought against this on the grounds that the public schools did not have the authority to confer an adult sexual identity upon minors. The charges against us? That we were intolerant and small-minded, insensitive to the needs of children. Yet it is precisely my love of children that compels me to combat the cruelty of assigning the label of "homosexual" to them.

Our world is becoming increasingly "gay friendly." In politics, education and the media we are barraged by the power of the "gay self." That self demands recognition and acceptance.

This is also a profoundly spiritual battle, one in which even the church seems confused and impotent. For that reason God in his mercy and truthfulness is raising up an army of men and women who can proclaim and impart the transforming power of Jesus Christ. This includes not only those from homosexual backgrounds but also men and women who stand with them in their healing journey. Mediating truth and grace, these supportive ones are crucial in helping the homosexually vulnerable to grasp the power of God amid their weakness.

Toward that end, we need to be equipped for the battle. First we must identify the enemy. It is not a political party, the wayward church or culture, or the gay community. There is only one enemy: Satan himself, the deceiver and robber of humanity. "He is a liar and the father of lies" and he seeks to destroy the gullible with his lies (Jn 8:44; 10:10). And there is only one goal—the saving of lives from an identity that distorts the essence of one's humanity.

POWER OF THE "GAY SELF"

I am convinced that the enemy empowers and employs the homosexual confusion in our culture to seduce men and women into embracing the "gay self." One cannot negate the spiritual deception that occurs when a person identifies with his or her homosexuality as the real, authentic self. Soon to follow will be a yielding to homosexual activity. The person's sexual desires are then strengthened as a result of his or her behaviors.[6]

One cannot dismiss the spiritual darkness at work in the lives of young, vulnerable men and women as "realized" homosexuals encourage their "true" gay selves. While at UCLA, I learned of several student meetings in which multiple invitations to embrace one's homosexuality were offered to incoming students. Several years later I had a dream of uncertain men and women with same-sex struggles entering that campus. As they sought out the gay student clubs, I could see them changing. Their lives were taking on new and perverse definition, all under the authority of the "gay self."

Spiritually, I knew that this new definition was empowered by the world, flesh and devil—it had nothing to do with the Creator's intentions for people. I cried out in my dream for God to raise a standard, in the hopes that the vulnerable might discover the true form God had in mind for them. But such empowerment can occur only if one has the grace and courage to admit one's struggle as a weakness rather than as a divine right. When the latter prevails, we witness the weakness of homosexuality becoming the ground of unholy power. The enemy empowers the "gay self" and distorts the core of one's humanity and spirituality.

Further empowering the "gay self" are the media-inspired assumptions that homosexuality is inborn and unchangeable, probably determined by a gay gene. Sound bites proclaim distorted and grossly oversimplified "facts" that no one with any scientific background would reasonably support as proof that one is born gay.

Complicating and reinforcing the issue is the assumption that homosexuals constitute a kind of ethnic minority. Many states have actually granted gays legal status on a par with non-Caucasians. I witnessed this deception firsthand when an African American man with a homosexual struggle accused me of seeking to annihilate his true self when I challenged his homosexual behavior on biblical grounds. He cited his black heritage as a corollary experience of oppression and striving for justice.

Assumptions about homosexuality as inborn are unfounded. Actual evidence for the origins of homosexuality support a multicausal base. Biology, family environment, culture and early sexual behavior all contribute to sexual development, but one's moral decision making determines sexual behavior, identity and lifestyle.

Still, the "gay self" will accept nothing other than the simplistic cop-out of biological destiny. This not only grants the homosexual immunity from moral decision making; it also buffers him or her from having to face the pain and wounding that underlies the same-sex struggle. The broken relational patterns that contribute to the development of homosexuality, including sexual abuse, parent-child issues, peer rejection and one's own conflicted response to these factors can thus be avoided.

The gay activist cannot frame his or her homosexuality as anything related to weakness, let alone brokenness. That would imply a need for healing. Instead she or he must assert the intrinsic wholeness of homosexuality. To reveal any crack in the gay armor would be to admit one's need to be saved.

To the "gay self," one need only be saved from those who challenge that self. The gay community gathers in solidarity to identify its enemies. At the forefront would be the church, or at least those churches that uphold God's image as male and female and place boundaries around sexual behavior. To gay activists, such a perspective is nothing short of abuse, a violation of the gay community. Even the most loving expression of such truth is considered unjust—an exclusive, outdated and prejudicial take on Scripture.

BLIND GUIDES

I bring up the cultural influences that empower the "gay self" for a simple reason—it is becoming increasingly difficult for Christians with same-sex tendencies to sort out the confusing signs and options related to homosexuality within our culture.

Imagine a young man beset by homosexual struggles. Unsure as to how or with whom to proceed, he looks outward to the media, silently scanning TV shows or magazine articles on the topic. Or maybe he will take it a step further and pursue counseling of some sort at university or in the community. The odds are, he will be encouraged to make peace with the struggle, to accept himself as intrinsically homosexual.

The church may mirror the world here. Many mainline churches are supportive of homosexuality; that's not a surprise. But even many evangelical churches are now wondering whether those with same-sex struggles can or should be directed onto the path of transformation.

I recently met with a bestselling evangelical writer whose references to homosexuality in his work concerned me in their ambiguity. As I investigated further, I discovered that this leader was actively supporting gay Christian couples. When we talked, he was upset at my take on Scripture, homosexuality and healing, and was equally upset that I could grasp his position from reading his books. (I guess he did not want to get into trouble with his publisher.)

I believe we will continue to see the growth of the gay Christian movement—men and women in the evangelical community who are seeking and finding empowerment in their homosexuality.

Deceptive signposts in the world and in the church obscure the clear path of redemption for the same-sex struggler. In so doing, these false guides contribute to the spiritual warfare that harasses young men and women in their sexual vulnerabilities. The "gay self" looms as a tempting and powerful solution to the struggle at hand.

That's why homosexual strugglers must establish roots in a healing community. They cannot afford to be silent about their struggle. They need those who can stand with them, aware of the vulnerability and the battle. Without that clear communal support, same-sex strugglers run the risk of falling prey to a culture in confusion. With that community, however, God can liberate a new creation whose magnificence puts the "gay self" to shame.

CONVERSION OF THE WILL

We need the community of the cross in order to emerge out of homosexuality. Such freedom involves a radical response to the One who calls us to deny ourselves, take up our cross daily and follow him (Lk 9:23). That response must involve Jesus' conversion of our wills—a persistent willingness to die to falsehood and embrace what is real and true. The process of dying in order to live—the cross-centered lifestyle—has everything to do with discipleship. Embracing the rhythm of the cross occurs over time as we submit ourselves to Christ and to one another.

Radical? Yes. But thoroughly biblical and normative for all Christians. Christ's call to give up everything for him—to lay our identities, our affections, our relationships on the line for the kingdom's sake—applies to all who claim to be Christian. That is where the healing of the homosexual prophetically addresses all of us. In order to get free, he or she must identify wholly with Christ and so be transformed. And this involves a conversion of the will.

Jesus asks the homosexually vulnerable, "Will you follow me or the worldly, demonic forces vying for your soul?" Precisely because of the power of those forces, Jesus appeals to the will. True conversion always involves such an appeal. Until the Lord has our wills, we are not truly converted.

This came clearly to my mind while I was leading a young man to Christ. He was in the midst of discovering the powerful passions available to him in the homosexual community. He wanted me to pray for his healing from homosexuality. But Jesus gently reminded me of the powerful idols that would still beckon to this young man after the prayer time. Jesus wanted his full allegiance. So I spoke these words gently and firmly to the young man: "The things you yearn for homosexually will still be available to you after this prayer time. Choose this day whom you will serve: Jesus or the idol gods of this age." He chose Christ!

God wants our wills. And we each have a choice—to unite ourselves to Christ or to follow the broad path of sexual immorality. Thomas Schmidt said it brilliantly:

Moral questions have to do with the rightness or wrongness of my actions, regardless of the source or strength of my desires. Whatever I may attribute to my genes or to my parents or to my culture, none of them can force me, at the crucial moment, to turn a glance into a fantasy, or a fantasy into a flirtation, or a flirtation into a sexual act. At that moment, my *will* is involved, and precisely such moments define my obedience and growth as a Christian.[7]

One skeptical young woman asked me, "In light of such struggle to make the right choice, is there real healing for the homosexual, real hope for change?" I thought for a moment about all the choices, all the battles I had endured. I responded to her as genuinely as I could. "Jesus always gives us the choice to fall forward. In our weakness we can fall backward into sin or forward into him."

To me the cross signifies the vital, healing center onto which I fall continuously. Christ has made a way for me in my weakness. Every hungry glance, every desire, every unmet yearning has a place in his heart. As I have discovered him in my weakness and have surrendered my homosexual struggle to him, he has been faithful. He has raised up in me a new heart, one capable of loving others well.

A homosexual struggler conveyed well the power of the cross in overcoming homosexuality.

There's a call going out, a cry sounding in hearts today, that is a courage, empowered by God's grace, to seek the Lord with everything, nothing in reserve, forsaking one's own life to attain

189

the inheritance of God. Sound familiar? Men and women coming out of homosexuality are part of this new breed that truly
and personally understand the message of the cross. Die to yourself and you will live. Jesus' words to deny myself once sounded
a bit extreme, but now I know they are the only hope of my sur-
vival. If I die to 99% of my old ways and passions, eventually that
1% will cost me my life—the real life God intends for all his children.

God will resurrect a new man or woman only after there has
been this death. Many people want to just bleed, enough to be
incapacitated, but not enough to die. The cross bids you to die.[8]

HEALING AT THE CROSS

Three points about conversion at the foot of the cross bear mention-
ing here. Two involve dying; the last, resurrection—the promise of
new life.

All three points reflect the truth that healing occurs at the cross, but
not on our terms. As Norvene Vest wrote, "True transformation follows God's ways, which are built into the structure of creation and
modeled for us in the life of Christ. True transformation leads from
death into life. We cannot willingly die by ourselves, so we seek . . .
to become like Christ and to receive his life in order to follow him
through the narrow door of death that leads to abundant life."[9] The
cross reveals God's intention and timing for our release.

Our first death involves surrendering the desire to lead a pain-free
life. We come out of denial and choose to face the pain of our lives.
Speaking to the homosexually vulnerable, we die to the lie that we
were born gay and are intrinsically homosexual. We instead seek the
grace and truth necessary to look at and accept our broken histories.
We then invite Christ and others to meet us in the shame and pain.
As Jesus begins to heal the wounded areas with his love, the force of
our homosexual affections decreases; we rightfully regard our same-
sex attachments as a distorted (though understandable) effort to se-

cure love from our own gender.

The second point of conversion involves dying to our tendency to make others our saviors. Here we face the hard truth that no one but Jesus can save us from our loneliness. No one person exists as the lost mother or father of our youth or as the special friend who is going to exclusively mediate the love we need. We face our selfishness and choose to die to it. Karl Rahner referred to this surrender as the cross of everyday life, "because in order to be utterly destroyed our selfishness must be ceaselessly crucified."[10]

This may involve grieving over the ones we must lay down at the cross. But let us take heart! The fruit of such dying "will be a love born from the death of our selfishness."[11] Freed from our grasping, we come with open hands and hearts to give to others. And we receive gratefully what they can give. We are thankful for their offering, however incomplete it is, as we no longer need this other to complete us.

Resurrection follows such dying. Jesus imparts new life to us as we emerge out of the "gay self" and into the new creation. We agree with the apostle Paul when he said, "May I never boast except in the cross. . . . What counts is a new creation" (Gal 6:14-15). That new life includes taking one's place as a part of God's heterosexual order. We are weak and vulnerable in unique ways, yet we stand upright according to his creative intentions for us—male and female.

POWER OF THE KINGDOM NOW

It is nothing less than the resurrection power of Jesus Christ that liberates us to take a stand for God's image as male and female. This is at once a positional authority and one granted us by the rule and reign of God's kingdom come in Christ. Jesus proclaimed the power of the Father breaking into the human realm. Through his Spirit, the very Spirit that raised Jesus from the tomb, the Father breaks the dominating power of our brokenness. This is God's kingdom come on earth— one that he is pleased to give us today (Lk 12:32).

Jesus' references to the kingdom are usually associated with acts of healing and deliverance (for example, Lk 10:9-11). The kingdom involves active demonstrations of God-with-us—his Spirit moving in extraordinary ways to set us free. The kingdom reality should provoke our expectancy. God wills to acts powerfully on our behalf to demonstrate his reign in Christ.

Jesus embodies the transforming power of God's presence in human history. He is in our midst now, wanting to enter and alter our personal histories with his healing power. Consequently God invites us to live expectantly; we await and discover his kingdom breaking into our lives afresh. Through his Spirit he transforms us more fully into his image and likeness. Homosexuality may have limited us in the past, but God breaks in and grants us kingdom power with which to live differently.

I have seen God act marvelously in the lives of ex-gays who were not expecting God to break in and reveal their true heterosexual potential. Frank Worthen, beloved pioneer and grandfather of ex-gay ministry, had become a solid man in Christ, light-years away from his decades of involvement in the gay life. But he settled on singleness. God had other plans. Well past middle age, Frank discovered through a variety of signs that God had marriage in store for him. He met and married Anita, and together the two have not ceased to bear fruit for God's kingdom.

God invites us in our homosexual vulnerability to discover the cross. He beckons us with his love and lays claim to our will. United with his loving will, we refuse the lies—worldly icons that fire up the "gay self," illusions of wholeness that underlie that "gay self," selfish expectations of others. We die, but such surrender is holy ground for the resurrection God has in store for us. He grants us new life and continuously pours out that new life in creative, even unexpected ways.

THE CROSS AND DISCIPLESHIP

The cross teaches us that death precedes life. As we die to our weakness, vulnerabilities may remain, but we have an advocate in the One. We fall forward and each time discover fresh grace and transforming power with which to arise. Such a crosswalk requires a track on which we can learn this vital rhythm of death unto life. That's where discipleship comes in. And that's where the healing of the homosexual reveals the need for time and instruction in order to become authentically Christian.

Transformation occurs as we learn to follow Christ. We grow in our ability to grasp the meaning of the cross—to welcome holy love, to surrender, to live. Dallas Willard recognized how "consumer Christianity" fails us here. He asserted that our main model in the church today is the seeker-sensitive one in which we utilize "the grace of God for forgiveness and the services of the church for special occasions, but [do] not give [our] lives and innermost thoughts, feelings, and intentions over to the kingdom of the heavens. Such Christians are not inwardly transformed and not committed to it."[12]

The healing of the homosexual requires an in-depth model of discipleship. There is no other way that we can be changed. Jesus makes the way for us—crucifixion unto resurrection. That truth becomes a living reality only as we commit ourselves to him and those who can help us. In that process he converts our will and transforms our very beings. Again, this reality should be normative for all Christians. For the homosexual seeking healing, it is nonnegotiable.

A HUMBLE REVOLUTION

God meets us at our point of greatest vulnerability and does his deepest work there. Those coming out of homosexuality can testify of this healing boldly and authentically. God is forging a cross-centered people who will stand amid great moral darkness and reveal the way of truth, not in theological abstractions but with the witness of their lives.

This witness of transformation has relevance to a dying, deceived world. That world is increasingly captivated by the proclaimed legitimacy of the "gay self." Who better to proclaim the power of dying to the "gay self" in order to truly live than those who have themselves gone through that death?

God reclaims us so that we can help reclaim others. With the cross before us, we can see what he sees in the gay community—a people "harassed and helpless, like sheep without a shepherd" (Mt 9:36). We can proclaim what he has done in our lives. We thus empower others to uphold the truth of what Jesus can do as they surrender to him. The culture wars over sexuality and homosexuality need compassionate, truthful voices. "By the word of [our] testimony" (Rev 12:11), the victory of the cross in our lives initiates that victory in others.

Tolstoy described the violent revolutions of history. I believe the sexual revolution of our day is violent in its own right, desecrating God's image in humanity. But Tolstoy also observed that God is faithful amid such violence. The great Russian writer acknowledged Van Gogh's perceived "private and secret revolution[s]" in which God heals and renews willing hearts. In the wake of violence, new life emerges through the revolutionary love of Jesus Christ.[13] Healed homosexuals are a part of this quiet revolution.

And this revolutionary witness has relevance to the church of Jesus Christ. As we have seen, the church often mirrors the world in its distorted take on homosexuality. Some expressions of the body dismiss gays; others embrace the "gay self" truthlessly. The church needs the witness of our transformation. In this way we reinforce her true inheritance as a healing, humble community. And we raise up the standard of discipleship, centered on the cross. That has been our cure—a cure relevant to all who truly want to follow Christ.

The challenge lies in the residual weaknesses that remain in the homosexual struggler. How can we carry out such a task in light of ongoing vulnerabilities? Strength in weakness. As we are faithful to carry the cross in times of victory and hard struggle, we become trustworthy disciples, increasingly dependent upon our healer, Jesus Christ. We become those "whose weakness was turned to strength; and who became powerful in battle and routed foreign armies" (Heb 11:34).

The Lord spoke through Anglican minister Andrew Beel to reveal more about this army. While praying for the forces of perversion to be overcome in his native Australia, Andrew received a vision. He saw a broken army, moving in nearly perfect harmony with its leader, the Lord of hosts. The ragged soldiers were impressive for only one reason—their obedience and utter reliance upon the Lord of glory. They marched according to the cadence of his heartbeat. His glory reflected upon the troops to such an extent that the army became radiant in his holiness. In fact, they were so dazzling that their reflected glory nearly blinded the enemy; he could no longer target them effectively. His efforts to divide and weaken the army failed. The troops advanced successfully wherever the Lord of glory led.

This is how darkness is overcome. In our weakness we cleave to the light and become strong. May we as a healing army march in unison with the Lord of glory. Let us fulfill together Paul's words when he exhorted us to "become blameless and pure, children of God without fault in a crooked and depraved generation, in which you shine like stars in the universe as you hold out the word of life" (Phil 2:15-16).

10

∽∿∽

THE CHURCH AT THE CROSS

The other day I was working out in the gym. While I was taking care of my body, God reminded me that the night before, Annette had barely slept due to some anxieties. She arose that day tense and physically depleted. These verses came to mind: "Husbands ought to love their wives as their own bodies. He who loves his wife loves himself. After all, no one ever hated his own body, but he feeds and cares for it, just as Christ does the church" (Eph 5:28-29).

While sweating and straining over my own body, I had neglected hers. I realized that I had failed to pray with her on behalf of some emotional and physical weaknesses she possesses. (I used to do this for her constantly in our early days or marriage—a service that God used to free her significantly.) The Father stirred me to forsake my selfishness and release his power to serve her in love. That day I resumed my prayerful care of the one I love most.

As we take Paul's words in Ephesians 5 seriously, I believe we can find another meaning in that text. Ephesians 5:25-29 describes Jesus' devotion to his beloved one—the church. I believe he wants us to possess that devotion as well. As we seek after his heart, we will discover ardent passion for the bride he is preparing for himself.

God is answering my prayers to possess more of his heart for his body. I ask him to show me what he sees when he looks at her. Just as I sometimes fail to love my wife aright and to treat her accordingly, so do I often fail to see and to serve the church in a manner that pleases him. But God willingly shows me the love for his church that is always pouring from his heart.

For Annette and me, our ministry to the broken has always flowed out of our local church involvement. As long-standing servants in the Vineyard Christian Fellowship, a church planting movement, we have helped pioneer several new churches. These were small, brave works in urban settings. The workers, including Annette and me, were a scrappy lot. The work was hard, the money was scarce and the needs of the broken were so great that it was easy to lose compassion.

One Sunday I was particularly weary and thus prone to petty judgments, but I prayed, "God, give me your heart for these ones today!" Then I spied from a distance a band of churchgoers. They were a ragged lot, but for a few moments God granted me his sight. I saw a royal procession before me, each one noble, marching regally together in crowns and gowns of the highest order. I saw them as God destined them to be—"a chosen people, a royal priesthood, a holy nation, a people belonging to God" (1 Pet 2:9).

God strengthens the weak to love his church. Indeed the weak possess a unique authority to serve the body. Perhaps it is because they know who their source of strength is. They gather to meet him and they serve him by serving one another. When they weary at doing well, they know their advocate. The same source that met them in their powerlessness over abuse, addiction or homosexuality enables them to give that power away. Personal and interpersonal weakness brought them to their knees; in holy power they arise, not merely to "get better" but to help strengthen others.

RECEIVING AND RELEASING MERCY

We receive God's mercy, and in so doing we become the church. We then seek to build the church as we take our rightful places as "a people belonging to God." The two rhythms occur simultaneously—we receive and we give. Our empowerment in weakness deepens, as does our service of the body. I see this, for example, in a dear friend of mine named Gary.

Gary is an alcoholic. Nine years sober, yet still weak, he rarely ceases to build up the body. Though our weaknesses differ, we meet on the ground of our need for daily bread. He hungers for the Word, receives it and gives it away freely. Rarely have I witnessed one whose weakness has become a source of such powerful love, beginning with his family and then fanning out to the church. I am one who has fed on the Word that has come through him, building me up in Christ and removing the threat of alienation and isolation. Such "repeated acts of community life," to borrow the words of Ray Anderson, have helped lay a sure foundation of God's mercy in me.[1]

Perhaps this sort of freedom to help bridge the gap for others in the church stems from ongoing experiences of God's mercy. Those who have known alienation—and its cure—may be the best priests. It may be as simple as what God said to the Israelites as they prepared to enter the land: "You are to love those who are aliens, for you yourselves were aliens in Egypt" (Deut 10:19). Those released from slavery become liberators for others.

Compassion received and released—the apostle Paul exemplified this essential rhythm of "body building" as he addressed the broken and deceived church at Corinth.

AFFLICTION AND COMPASSION

Conflicts within the church brought suffering to Paul. But that suffering gave rise to rich consolation and compassion from the Father. Paul welcomed that comfort in his own distress. He then sought to address the church out of the compassion he had received. This word begins the letter, as it should rightfully begin our service of healing for the broken body:

> Praise be to the God and Father of our Lord Jesus Christ, the Father of compassion and the God of all comfort, who comforts us in all our troubles, so that we can comfort those in any trouble

with the comfort we ourselves have received from God. For just as the sufferings of Christ flow over into our lives, so also through Christ our comfort overflows. (2 Cor 1:3-5)

Paul discovered affliction in his passion for the bride. More than that, he discovered the compassion of the One who loved through him. Suffering for the people gave rise to greater love for them. Instead of inciting rage or even control, Paul's distress became the ground for powerful grace. That spirit pervaded Paul's tone as he addressed the crisis at hand. He freely admitted his weaknesses, then ended his letter with powerful, authoritative love.

Paul's response to the Corinthians can be a model for us as we seek to love the church. Like the apostle, we begin by acknowledging that we are a part of the body—we are weak and desperately in need of the Lord and one another. This releases grace for the church, tender mercies with which to love her. We also, like Paul, can welcome suffering on behalf of the church. We can proceed in the confidence that Jesus is forging his way, the way of the cross, into our hearts through such trials. And last, like Paul, we can expect powerful love to arise in us as we take our places as "body builders." Secure in our servant authority, we assert Christ's grace and truth and transforming power in the body to prepare her for his return.

WE ARE THE BRIDE

Our commitment to loving the church begins with our identifying ourselves as a part of her. It defies the very nature of how Jesus sees us to try to separate ourselves from the church. He sees us individually, yet he is restoring us as part of a much greater whole—the bride for whom he is returning.

Still, many of us may seek to distance ourselves from this family on the basis of her brokenness. We may even equate the local Christian body with our troubled natural families—unsafe, not deserving of our trust. And to be sure, the church is broken. Nevertheless, we cannot do as we may have done with our natural families and seek to disassociate from her. We must make peace with her. We must also face our part in the family's brokenness and become a part of her cure.

I was reminded of this once when I was in Copenhagen, Denmark, preaching at a Lutheran church. I was there at the request of the pastor, Ole Mogensen, who is a good friend of mine. Ole wanted me to speak to his congregation because they were going through a crisis related to a devastating moral failure.

While preaching, I noticed a huge painting near the altar. It depicted a bride lying in the mud, her bridal gown stained and torn by what appeared to be a fall. She seemed mournful and humiliated, as if aware that she was out of place. She looked like a woman who had wandered from her betrothed and was now regretting it. But awareness of her disorientation did not restore her. She needed holy rescue. This woman, of course, was the bride of Christ—the church.

As I reflected upon my experience with the body of Christ, both locally and internationally, I concurred with her brokenness. More than that, I recalled her resilience. Through her Bridegroom she possesses an infinite capacity for renewal. This battered bride possesses a Groom who "gave himself up for her," who perseveres in love in order to wash her, who will stop at nothing "to present her to himself as . . . radiant . . . without stain or wrinkle or any other blemish" (Eph 5:25-27).

She is us. In our thoughts and feelings, our interpersonal actions and reactions to fellow Christians, our attachments to people and institutions, we represent a part of the muddy bride. Our devotion to Christ and to our fellow Christians is partly pure, partly defiled. Our efforts at loving others have left us alternately empowered and wrung out.

Like Paul, we are wholly dependent upon Christ to strengthen us. The afflictions we sustain as his bride—"conflicts on the outside, fears within" (2 Cor 7:5)—require holy washing and comfort. Such affliction applies to the range of issues we have discussed in this book:

shame over our brokenness, sins we conceive in our weakness, the wounding we incur from others' sin and finally the weakness (or "thorn") itself.

God in his mercy frees us to be his broken body. We need not run from that pronouncement nor hate ourselves for it. In truth, to hate the bride for her weakness and failures is to hate ourselves.

Perhaps we face the same temptation that Peter did when Jesus knelt to wash the disciples' feet. Peter was outraged at his Master's suggestion, since in that day feet were considered the humblest part of the human body. Jesus responded to Peter's refusal to submit his feet to Jesus for washing by saying, "Unless I wash you, you have no part with me" (Jn 13:8).

We can readily apply this washing to the multiple weaknesses, wounds and wickedness that mark our "family" gathering. All that Jesus requires of us is the recognition and extension of our dirty feet. Will we dare to present them to him? If we will, he will be pleased. He welcomes such humility, and there he will be faithful to wash us—to comfort us, to cleanse us, to empower us to love far beyond our natural capacity.

Much of this washing will occur as we gather together. He restores us through his bride as she is being healed. Paul relied upon his healing band to mediate God's strength in his weakness. Right after lamenting his affliction, he rejoiced by saying, "God, who comforts the downcast, comforted us by the coming of Titus" (2 Cor 7:6). Likewise, God meets us through trustworthy agents of mercy. We need safe places in the body where we can reveal our dirty feet, knowing we will receive comfort and cleansing, not further humiliation.

That is especially true for Christian leaders.

LEADERS NEED WASHING

It is no easy thing for spiritual parents to submit their weaknesses to others. In part this is due to the need for boundaries—those we serve should not be expected to bear our burdens. But as leaders, where are our peer relationships? Often they are lacking.

In serving others, we must admit that over time the door of our hearts may have come to open only one way—outward. We may have lost the sense of freedom to allow others in. The truth is, the more responsibility we have, the more we need others. We must cultivate those peer relationships with others who do not need for us to be the leader. In so doing, we assert our freedom be a part of the muddy bride, willingly exposing our feet to trustworthy others for washing.

I am encouraged by increasing numbers of Christian leaders who gather for the sake of healing and cleansing. Jesus comes quickly to wash and empower his leaders in their humiliation. Nothing is nearer his heart than tending to his muddy shepherds via these particular expressions of the body.

The fruit of such washing is apparent. One becomes clean via the mercy of God. The leader rediscovers grace, not as an abstraction, but as the basis for his or her salvation and calling. The leader can then begin to reestablish integrity in relationships where there has been compromise. God digs a deeper well of compassion in him or her for other members of the muddy bride. They can comfort others authentically with the comfort they have received. Like Paul, these freshly washed shepherds display the "unlimited patience" of Jesus "as an example for those who would believe on him and receive eternal life" (1 Tim 1:16).

Our first task as leaders, then, is to identify with the muddy bride— we are her. We discover in our fellow believers the grace we need. This, in turn, looses a fresh stream of grace for others.

But we must also be willing to persevere with the bride, even to suffer on her behalf. This is our second task. When we choose to endure misunderstanding, even injustice, in our church relationships, Jesus takes us deeper into his heart. I believe we become uniquely identified with him when we suffer for doing right on behalf of his body.

SUFFERING FOR WHAT IS RIGHT

Holy suffering is a mark of spiritual maturity. At the beginning of our healing journeys, we learn to identify those who have sinned against us. We process the emotions; we learn to speak the truth in love to our offenders. Here we often face the temptation to undue reactivity, even to assume the identity of "victim." But we must grow beyond that identification. If we are faithful to do so, we will realize another kind of suffering. This is the suffering for doing what is right. As we take our places as whole-enough healers in the body, we discover that some do not like our offering, the unique expressions of the body that we are becoming.

I see this clearly in men and women who are recovering from various forms of brokenness. Through ministries like Desert Stream they find a particular grace and freedom. But this kind of ministry may not yet be normative in their churches. Full of gratitude and enthusiasm, these people struggle to understand why their own church is hesitant to embrace the "foot washing" that has set them free. They may find indifference, even antagonism toward in-depth healing. How we persevere amid such resistance may determine whether or not our church ever opens up to the prospect of such ministry. We pray; we wait; we serve.

Other types of resistance from the church are even more profound and painful. That's what Kin and Jolene Lancaster discovered when they became senior leaders at a church. They were open about their histories—Kin's homosexuality, an adulterous affair early on in their marriage, Jolene's history of sexual abuse and profound physical and emotional suffering in the marriage. Having both received much healing, they accepted the post based upon a commitment to being honest about their past. They did so in the hope of extending ministry to broken ones in the church.

A couple of church leaders grew resentful and resistant to the "inner healing" emphasis of the new pastors. They began to circulate rumors about the couple, using their histories against them. Kin and Jolene had to continue to lead the church in light of divisiveness and deception. Kin was tempted to use the pulpit to blast these leaders out of the church. Instead they pressed on with the church in light of what God had called them to do. At the right time Kin and Jolene would deal with the deceivers individually, but in the meantime they allowed the Lord to take them deeper in his suffering while they awaited justice.

HOSTILE TO HEALING

We must face honestly the truth that some conservative communities of faith can be hostile to healing ministry. They react to the threat of sexual brokenness by closing their doors on the broken. They often love a form of truth but have employed it abusively, without grace. They "load people down with burdens they can hardly carry," while they "will not lift one finger to help them" (Luke 11:46).

Sonja Stark suffered under one such church. Her pastors cut her out of their community because they worried about her struggle with sexual fantasies for men in their congregation. Afraid that Sonja's struggle would create problems in the church, they left her to persevere alone instead of helping her to find healing. Sonja began to feel as though God too had left her to struggle on her own.

Although she has since reconciled with that church, overcoming her fear of abandonment caused by her experience was a long process. Her healing occurred in a new community of faith in which pastors and members alike modeled a freedom to deal honestly with brokenness. Over time her vision of church life and leadership has been transformed. Sonja now freely and effectively equips pastors throughout Europe to heal the broken in their congregations.

The church can also err in another direction. In the name of "love" some churches extend their holy covering over all manner of moral wickedness, including premarital sex, multiple partnerships and homosexual practices. These churches mislead the servants of God into sexual immorality (Rev 2:20-29). They may even seek to penalize those who are committed to the biblical parameters that reserve sexual practice for marriage.

In North America and Europe pastoral colleagues of mine are losing status and privilege in their churches for their commitment to biblical sexuality, including the healing of the homosexual. Certain
branches of the body of Christ have become so dominated by gay or
gay-sympathetic clergy that those who feel differently are shamed into
silence. Those who dare speak out for healing are denied opportunities
to serve to their fullest potential.

In seeking a parish position, one Anglican priest and Living Waters
leader received no real options from the bishop, a man surrounded by
gay priests. Another Lutheran colleague—a deacon in the church for
decades—was forbidden in his denomination from sharing about the
healing of the homosexual. I met with a well-known Catholic cardi-
nal who, though sympathetic to our ministry and theologically
aligned with us, presided over a national church structure dominated
by gay priests. To take a redemptive stand on the issue—even one in
line with the church's teaching—would have been too costly for him
politically.

COURAGE TO STAND

In some mainline churches we witness the power of entrenched sexual
immorality, including homosexual practice. Those who choose to
stand for the truth will pay—in reputation and in status. It will require
dying to the perverse traditions of men. Yet some manage to find the
needed courage.

One fine pastor and colleague of mine faced a huge challenge.
Centered in a city famous for its sexual license, his church was rife
with immorality. At the same time the congregation exhibited a nearly
pharisaic refusal to deal honestly and forthrightly with its brokenness.
He struggled in his efforts to provide a clear path of redemption for
the people.

He courageously invited me to come and share my story, telling
how Jesus invites us to face our sin so that he can empower us to grow

into his best for us. At the end of my talk, before a rather impassive congregation of five hundred members, I called forward those in need of the greater power of God in any weakness related to their sexuality. Twelve men and women bravely approached the front. I prayed for them. We wept together as if no one else was there.

Then the pastor came forward and wisely told his congregation, "Seventy-five percent of you needed that prayer. These courageous ones have chosen the greater thing this day. And as a result of their courage, they shall serve you Communion." He broke the elements, distributed them to the twelve and then had them turn around to the church in order to dispense the holy meal for all.

Afterward many in his church blasted the pastor. Yet he stood firm in raising the standard of grace and truth.

This pastor, and many like him, are raising such a standard in their churches. That standard is nothing less than the cross of Jesus Christ, full of grace and truth. To plant the cross, we must also be willing to bear the cross. We will suffer for what is right. We endure such suffering for Christ's sake, dying to our "rights" while cleaving to the truth. He teaches us of his cross in new ways as we choose to carry that cross through church-based suffering. The result? A remnant of holy truth that will endure in his church, making a way for the healing of the faithful.

CARRYING MY CROSS

The apostle Paul showed us how to carry the cross of suffering on behalf of Christ's body. In those times Jesus calls us to quiet our hearts and press into him. Like Paul, we die to our own resurrection schemes—the clamor of personal rights and privileges. There have been a couple of times in my life that God has called me to put myself in a hard place for the sake of the church, and I've experienced this kind of suffering.

The first occasion involved a beloved elder with whom I labored in tending to the church. A single man, he was intent on marrying, so he rightfully dated. But in his dating relationships he began to cross certain lines, emotionally and physically, with a series of women from the church. I became aware of this pattern and assessed it as nothing short of spiritual abuse, due to his position with the church.

After observing several dealings this elder had with women whom he had romanced and then dropped for another, I challenged him. I told him that he needed to inform his overseer as to how he was handling his sexuality in the context of the church. He refused. I then went to his overseer. Although initially open to my concerns, the overseer allowed the elder to refute my claims. It all became my problem—first with the elder, then with the overseer, then with the entire leadership team of our church. I became the bad guy! I was asked to leave the church and was deemed a religious legalist, ungrateful for all that the elder and church had done for me.

Annette and I and the whole Desert Stream staff suffered. For the first time we were spiritually homeless. I thought our time as a ministry was over. But God took us deeper, calling us to trust him and to forgive all those who had rejected us for our position. We strove to do so.

We began to attend another church. Two years later a couple of women voiced their complaint about the elder's violations. This time the overseer listened and the elder was removed.

The next incident involved a man in our ministry who sexually violated a teenager. His abuse incurred a huge lawsuit against the ministry and the church. Our church at the time had a new pastor who was uncertain as to how Desert Stream fit into the context of the church. Though we had served there a long time, our future seemed to hang in the balance. The lawsuit—a potential threat to the church's financial well-being—tipped the scales.

Our pastor decided to shut down all the inner-healing groups offered by the church, including those related to our ministry. Many church members began to express their discontent with us. Several made it clear that our offering should not be a part of this or any church's mission.

It became a struggle to even attend our church. One Sunday I arrived and saw that all of our ministry's materials had been removed from the church. That night I received a phone call from a pastor friend of mine who said it was "unsafe" for his church to sponsor one of our healing groups at his church due to what was happening in our congregation. My heart felt sick. My spiritual home had once again become a place of sorrow and rejection.

Though I wanted to react, God called me to obey him. I urged all of the Desert Stream staff to pray for our pastor, who had to sort out what to do amid the legal and financial crises at hand. We also had to release those who in this time of trial revealed their true colors as adversaries of our work.

We prayed and waited. Had we reacted and left the church for the sake of "justice," we would have disobeyed the Lord of justice. He reminded us that he was still there in the church. He called us to stand quietly, to worship him and to build up his body. He assured us that he would serve justice his way.

God did more in that season to deepen my love for the church than in any other. I realized that my love for her needed to be tested in order to become truer, deeper and less reactive. In that season of censure God was refining my love for the bride.

STANDING IN LOVE

Out of both situations (and many other smaller trials we faced in the church), God called us to stand in his love and in the authority he had granted us on behalf of the body. As we faced the scrutiny of the created, we had to press into the Creator. He shored up our foundations as the ministry of his design—one called to wash the feet of Christ's body. He shored up our commitment to the truth that exposes sin and to the grace that cleanses us.

These words of Isaiah on behalf of his exiled nation became my own in these seasons. I considered the brokenness of Christ's body—her state of "exile" in light of the sin and wounding she bore. And I asked for God's power in my weakness to endure trials for her sake.

For Zion's sake I will not keep silent,
for Jerusalem's sake I will not remain quiet,
till her righteousness shines out like the dawn,
her salvation like a blazing torch.
The nations will see your righteousness,
and all kings your glory;
you will be called by a new name
that the mouth of the LORD will bestow.
You will be a crown of splendor in the LORD's hand,
a royal diadem in the hand of your God. . . .
I have posted watchmen on your walls, O Jerusalem;
they will never be silent day or night.
You who call on the LORD,
give yourselves no rest,
and give him no rest till he establishes Jerusalem
and makes her the praise of the earth. (Is 62:1-3, 6-7)

Our standing firm paid off. In the first crisis involving the compromising elder, God assured me that my concern for the well-being of the women in that church was more important than pleasing any one person, including that elder. John Wimber, founder of the Vineyard movement, heard of our temporary state of homelessness as a ministry and decided to provide a home for us as well as multiple opportunities for our offering to go forth. The crisis that I believed could have been the death knell of our ministry thus resulted in our promotion. We took the next step up in building and blessing the body of Christ.

In the second situation God called us to die to any need for recognition and approval from the church. But out of that death God revived our powerful conviction of how important our offering was to the church. As we prayed, God challenged us with the truth that we were an intrinsic part of the bride—to leave her would cause suffering to the whole. So we grew in confidence that our part, namely the healing of sexual and relational brokenness, was vital to her well-being. We dug in our heels, asking God to empower us to keep believing in his best for the church.

After a couple of years, things changed quickly. The legal issues were settled and we as a ministry had gained fresh wisdom and protective boundaries to help avert future legal problems. The church leadership reintroduced our healing offering into its curriculum, and we as a staff forged new ties with the pastors. Many of our adversaries left the church. In reflecting upon the hard journey we had endured together, my pastor, Lance Pittluck, looked at me and said, "You passed the test"—not his testing of me, but God's testing. Our ministry remains at the Vineyard Anaheim, and our commitment to the church at large has never been more focused and fruitful. Suffering on behalf of the bride strengthened our love for her.

EMPOWERED TO SERVE

The apostle Paul arose in holy power amid the various afflictions he describes throughout his second letter to the Corinthians. In 2 Corinthians 10 we note a change in tone. Fueled by divine strength and armed in truth, the apostle calls the people to "demolish" the lies of the world that are infecting the church (10:3-5). He clearly states that in Christ he has knowledge far superior to the lies of the super-apostles (11:5-6). Paul then reminds the Corinthians of his weaknesses, describing the thorn in his flesh (11:16—12:10). Through it all, he points to God's power at work in him to empower the church.

We too may be acutely aware of weaknesses, but with our eyes on the One, we can continue to advance God's kingdom. There are three key areas that help us to be ready to serve.

First, we must find places in the church where we can deal with our brokenness. We need safe and trustworthy "foot washers" in order to become clean. Then, having received that mercy, we can authentically give it away to others. We will then fulfill Christ's words to his disciples: "Now that I, your Lord and Teacher, have washed your feet, you also should wash one another's feet" (Jn 13:14).

Second, we must expect to endure trials as we serve the broken bride. Although we choose to build up others in ways appropriate to our maturity and experience, we may find that we are not readily received. The church often reflects the world in its confusion over sexual and relational issues. On one hand, we may face the permissive church where truth has given way to falsehood, especially in regard to sexual immorality. On the other hand, churches rich in truth but rigid in practice may have little room for the messy humility required of those seeking in-depth healing.

Third, we experience God's strengthening so that we can persevere in loving and serving the church. In our day sexual and relational brokenness threaten to obscure the image of God in humanity. Such captivity is hell. It is authored and governed by evil. The one hope for the desecration of God's image in humanity is the church. She is the only gathering on earth against which the gates of hell will not prevail (Mt 16:18). We stand together as a humble and pure offering for the broken. We, like Paul, discover a deeper revelation of the cross in our bearing with the broken, beautiful bride. Out of those depths comes fresh water—truth, grace, healing power—with which to overcome evil with good.

STRENGTH IN WEAKNESS

The Father promises to strengthen fragile ones who place their trust in him and make their purpose the building up of his body on earth. Jesus exemplified strength in weakness at Calvary with his crucifixion unto resurrection. He makes us strong as we choose to stand. Our voices and legs may tremble in that choice. Many of us will even testify of that which has been shameful in our lives but that now proclaims his transforming power. Jesus is mightily revealed through humble, honest vessels. He richly fills such jars of clay.

The Father reiterates the truth of his Son's cross again and again as he empowers us in our weakness. He longs to do so. For his name's sake. On behalf of the church that bears his name. And on behalf of a world that will perish unless it finds refuge among us, the bride who is being healed. Let us take our places there, confident of his sufficiency to uphold us. Let us become his healers, doing our part as he empowers us in our weakness.

My grace is sufficient for you, for my power is made perfect in weakness. (2 Cor 12:9)

He is not weak in dealing with you, but is powerful among you. For to be sure, he was crucified in weakness, yet he lives by God's power. Likewise, we are weak in him, yet by God's power we will live with him to serve you. (2 Cor 13:3-4)

AFTERWORD

God revealed the strength of his love in my weakness one morning not long ago. Consider it a parable for what we all can experience in our relational or sexual brokenness.

I was attending a conference in England, and during a break I decided to go for a run in the countryside. Since I was an experienced runner and had even begun to compete in marathons, I felt sure of my capacity to do whatever I wanted on foot without ill consequences. And as this particular part of the world was comprised of small farms separated by fences, I began to run quickly through the fields, hurdling each fence that opposed me. As I hit my stride, I began to feel the "runner's high." I felt unstoppable.

Then I came to a taller fence, one that was about four feet high, consisting of two rows of barbed wire. Certain of my ability, I made a flying leap over the fence and for a second thrilled at the sight of my right leg sailing over it.

My left leg was not as successful. It got caught between the rows of wire, causing me to snap back from my one-legged landing. I hung there in shock and great pain, confused as to what to do. But then something like adrenaline kicked in and I wrenched my left leg out of its trap.

Immediately my mind signaled to my body that in spite of what had happened I could continue my run. As I raced off, I told myself, *What good will it do to stop and inspect my leg? That won't heal it. And besides, who will help me anyway, this presumptuous American, racing through other people's property?*

That logic held for about twenty-five paces until I felt something warm on my foot. A steady stream of blood was coursing down my injured leg and soaking my sock and shoe. I could feel a throbbing ache. I had no choice but to stop. In what I assume was a kind of prayer, I cried out, "What now?"

Just then, off to the right, I saw a small path that led toward an archway of trees. I hobbled over to the trees and discovered a beautiful stream. Immediately I took off my bloody shoe and sock and immersed my wounded leg in the clear water. It felt marvelous. As I rested I looked about me, enjoying the sunlight as it sifted through the trees and sparkled on the water.

Eventually the bleeding stopped. Indeed healing seemed to occur during every moment I spent immersed in that stream. After about forty-five minutes, though, I realized that I had to get out of the water and make my way back to my lodging.

As I was en route God whispered these words to me: "This is a glimpse of the power of my grace in your life. When you were young, you thought you could leap over every boundary line and get away with it. Even when the pain of your rebellion became apparent to you, you denied it. Only when the effects of sin showed themselves did you slow down long enough to listen.

"I led you to my Son, Jesus Christ, who from his cross released a flood of healing—blood for the forgiveness of sin and water for cleansing. When you called on his name, I loosed that cleansing flood over you. I sent faithful Christians to abide with you as that healing stream permeated every source of sin and shame. You—your old man, your old vision of yourself—died in the waters, and I raised you up in new life.

"Not only were your sins washed away, but I also cleansed your wounds. I gently bound up the brokenness inflicted on you. I washed away the shame you carried through others' rejection and abuse.

"And I freed you to be weak before me and others, not hard and defensive nor brash and foolish. I freed you to enter my pool of mercy again and again to receive grace to help you in your weakness. You learned to walk free from the shame and to receive mercy from fellow Christians as from my hand. And you grew and gained a vision of how my strength is available to you in your weakness.

"Every step of the way I am with you. I walked with you as you met Annette and got married. Your love for her is pure and powerful, full of passion, because I inhabit your union. And I have been with you as you have sought to parent your four children. I have fathered you and empowered you to father them.

"I know you are still weak. You still walk with a limp, a reminder of what I have saved you from and what I have saved you for—to call others into the river so that they too can arise as members of my healing army. But I have trained you to rely upon me and I have strengthened you at every step.

"Give freely to others the grace in which I have immersed you. Raise high the cross for all to see, for from my cross I release the cleansing, healing flood that is the hope for humanity. Only here can sin and shame and wounding be dissolved. Only here can my people be strengthened in their weakness and become fruitful agents of my kingdom. Only here can my sons and daughters learn how to love well, even as I have loved them."

Notes

Introduction

[1]Bonaventure, "The Soul's Journey into God," in *Bonaventure*, ed. and trans. Ewert Cousins (Mahwah, N.J.: Paulist, 1978), p. 54.

[2]Philip Edgcumbe Hughes, *Paul's Second Epistle to the Corinthians* (Grand Rapids, Mich.: Eerdmans, 1962), p. 230.

Chapter 1: God's Image in Humanity

[1]John Paul II, *The Theology of the Body: Human Love in the Divine Plan* (Boston: Pauline, 1997), p. 176.

[2]Donald Bloesch, *Is the Bible Sexist? Beyond Feminism and Patriarchalism* (Westchester, Ill.: Crossway, 1982), p. 24.

[3]John Paul II, *Theology of the Body*, p. 63.

[4]Ibid., p. 46.

[5]Ray Anderson, *On Being Human: Essays in Theological Anthropology* (Grand Rapids, Mich.: Eerdmans, 1982), p. 48.

[6]Ibid., p. 105.

[7]Andrew Comiskey, *Pursuing Sexual Wholeness: How Jesus Heals the Homosexual* (Lake Mary, Fla.: Creation House, 1989), pp. 109-25.

[8]John Paul II, *Theology of the Body*, p. 159.

[9]Karl Barth, *The Doctrine of Creation*, vol. 3 of *Church Dogmatics*, ed. G. W. Bromiley and T. F. Torrance (Edinburgh: T & T Clark, 1961), p. 156.

[10]Ibid., p. 159.

[11]Ibid., p. 163.

[12]Ibid., p. 164.

[13]Ibid.

[14]Ibid., p. 170.

[15]Anderson, *On Being Human*, p. 123. *Imago dei* is Latin for "image of God."

[16]Barth, *Doctrine of Creation*, p. 165.

[17]Ibid., p. 135.

[18]John Paul II, *Theology of the Body*, p. 81.

Chapter 2: Facing the Broken Image

[1]Ray Anderson, *On Being Human: Essays in Theological Anthropology* (Grand Rapids,

Mich.: Eerdmans, 1982), pp. 83-84.

[2]John Paul II, *The Theology of the Body: Human Love in the Divine Plan* (Boston: Pauline, 1997), p. 84.

[3]Susan T. Foh, "What Is the Woman's Desire?" *Westminster Theological Journal* 37, no. 3 (1975): 376-83.

[4]Victor Hamilton, *The Book of Genesis, Chapters 1–17* (Grand Rapids, Mich.: Eerdmans, 1990), p. 202.

[5]Karl Barth, *The Doctrine of Creation,* vol. 3 of *Church Dogmatics,* ed. G. W. Bromiley and T. F. Torrance (Edinburgh: T & T Clark, 1961), p. 178.

[6]Ibid.

[7]Ibid., pp. 179-80.

[8]John Paul II, *Theology of the Body,* p. 121.

[9]Barth, *Doctrine of Creation,* p. 133.

[10]John Paul II, *Theology of the Body,* p. 149.

[11]Lawrence J. Friesen, "Sexuality: A Biblical Model in Historical Perspective" (D.Min. diss., Fuller Theological Seminary, 1989), p. 193.

[12]Ibid., p. 96.

[13]John Paul II, *Theology of the Body,* p. 117.

[14]Barbara Dafoe Whitehead, *The Divorce Culture* (New York: Knopf, 1997), p. 19, as cited in Bridget Maher, "The Devastation of Divorce," Family Research Council: Marriage and Family (August 30, 2000) <www.frc.org/get/if00h2.cfm?CFID=895174&CFTOKEN=16291400>.

[15]Ibid.

[16]"Facts in Brief: Induced Abortion," Alan Guttmacher Institute (February 2000) <www.agi-usa.org/pubs/fb_induced_abortion.html>.

[17]Barth, *Doctrine of Creation,* p. 166.

[18]Reuters Health, reported March 14, 2001, online by Reuters Press, based on Amy C. Butler, "Trends in Same-Gender Partnering, 1988-1998," *Journal of Sex Research* 37 no. 4 (2000): 333-43.

[19]Quoted in Jeannine Stein, "Mixed Signals," *Los Angeles Times,* November 4, 1993, p. E1.

[20]Barth, *Doctrine of Creation,* p. 159.

[21]Mary McNamara, "Era of the Gender Crosser," *Los Angeles Times,* February 27, 2001, p. A20.

[22]Ibid.

Chapter 3: Strength to Love Well

[1]"The Year's Most Intriguing Findings," Barna Research Online (December 12, 2000) <http://216.87.179.136/cgi-bin/PagePressRelease.asp?PressReleaseID=77&References=F>.

[2]John R. W. Stott, *The Cross of Christ* (Downers Grove, Ill.: InterVarsity Press, 1986), p. 255.

[3]Jürgen Moltmann, *The Crucified God: The Cross of Christ as the Foundation and Criti-*

cism of Christian Theology, trans. R. A. Wilson and John Bowden (Minneapolis: Fortress, 1993), p. 7.

[4]Ibid., p. 204.

[5]Ibid., p. 212.

[6]Hans-Ruedi Weber, *The Cross: Tradition and Interpretation,* trans. Elke Jessett (Philadelphia: Westminster Press, 1979), p. 75.

[7]Edward J. Young, *Chapters 40—66,* vol. 3 of *The Book of Isaiah* (Grand Rapids, Mich.: Eerdmans, 1972), pp. 343-44.

[8]Moltmann, *Crucified God,* p. 312.

[9]C. S. Lewis, *Mere Christianity* (New York: Macmillan, 1952), p. 175.

[10]Karl Barth, *The Doctrine of Creation,* vol. 3 of *Church Dogmatics,* ed. G. W. Bromiley and T. F. Torrance (Edinburgh: Clark, 1961), pp. 167-68.

[11]Vincent Van Gogh, *The Letters of Vincent Van Gogh,* ed. Mark Roskill (London: Flamingo, 2000), p. 258.

[12]Donald Bloesch, *Is the Bible Sexist? Beyond Feminism and Patriarchalism* (Westchester, Ill.: Crossway, 1982), p. 24.

Chapter 4: Strength to Leave Shame Behind

[1]S. S. Tomkins, quoted in Gershen Kaufman, *The Psychology of Shame: Theory and Treatment of Shame-Based Syndromes,* 2d ed. (New York: Springer, 1996), p. 16.

[2]See Stephen Pattison, *Shame: Theory, Therapy, Theology* (Cambridge: Cambridge University Press, 2000), p. 93.

[3]John Paul II, *The Theology of the Body: Human Love in the Divine Plan* (Boston: Pauline, 1997), pp. 51-55.

[4]Karl Barth, cited in Pattison, *Shame,* p. 191.

[5]Ibid., p. 115.

[6]Ibid., p. 192.

[7]Ibid., p. 40.

[8]Ibid., p. 56.

[9]Kaufman, *Psychology of Shame,* p. 5.

[10]Pattison, *Shame,* p. 181.

[11]Kaufman, *Psychology of Shame,* p. 24.

[12]Ibid., p. 17.

[13]Erik Erikson, quoted in Pattison, *Shame,* p. 69.

[14]Pattison, *Shame,* p. 43.

[15]Ibid., p. 266.

[16]Ibid., p. 195.

[17]Kaufman, *Psychology of Shame,* p. 299.

[18]Ibid., p. 275.

[19]Ibid., p. 67.

[20]Pattison, *Shame,* p. 105.

[21]Ibid., p. 279.

[22]Kaufman, *Psychology of Shame,* p. 144.

[23]Pattison, *Shame,* p. 113.

[24]Ibid., p. 220.

[25]Dietrich Bonhoeffer, *Life Together,* trans. John W. Doberstein (San Francisco: Harper & Row, 1954), p. 20.

[26]Kaufman, *Psychology of Shame,* p. 159.

Chapter 5: Strength to Overcome Sin

[1]Dietrich Bonhoeffer, *Life Together,* trans. John W. Doberstein (San Francisco: Harper & Row, 1954), p. 110.

[2]Ibid.

[3]Ibid., p. 114.

[4]Ibid.

[5]Stephen Pattison, *Shame: Theory, Therapy, Theology* (Cambridge: Cambridge University Press, 2000), p. 168.

[6]Bonhoeffer, *Life Together,* p. 114.

[7]Ibid., pp. 116-17.

[8]Gene Edward Veith, "The Pornographic Culture," *World,* April 7, 2001, p. 17. Pornography was an $8 billion industry as of 1997 and no doubt has grown since then.

[9]Søren Kierkegaard, *Purity of Heart Is to Will One Thing,* trans. Douglas V. Steere (New York: Harper/Torchbooks, 1956), p. 47.

[10]I have found that the use of water makes apparent to the one confessing the reality of how God washes us in spirit and in truth. However, if such usage is a stumbling block to your Christian tradition, forget about the water. It is Christ alone who is the source of our forgiveness and cleansing; other helps, like the water, are expendable.

Chapter 6: Wounds That Heal

[1]Jürgen Moltmann, *The Crucified God: The Cross of Christ as the Foundation and Criticism of Christian Theology,* trans. R. A. Wilson and John Bowden (Minneapolis: Fortress, 1993), p. 277.

[2]Thomas Smail, *Windows on the Cross* (Boston: Cowley, 1996), p. 67.

[3]Moltmann, *Crucified God,* p. 195.

[4]Ibid., p. 205.

[5]Ibid., p. 149.

[6]Ibid., p. 148.

[7]Ibid., p. 243.

[8]Quoted in Kathleen Norris, *The Cloister Walk* (New York: Riverhead, 1996), p. 27.

[9]Moltmann, *Crucified God,* p. 245.

[10]Vincent Van Gogh, *The Letters of Vincent Van Gogh,* ed. Mark Roskill (Hammersmith, U.K.: Flamingo, 2000), pp. 118-19.

[11]Alan Paton, *Cry, the Beloved Country* (New York: Scribner, 1995), p. 261.

[12]Andrew Comiskey, *Living Waters: Pursuing Sexual and Relational Wholeness in Christ* (Anaheim, Calif.: Desert Stream Press, 2000), chapter seven.

[13]Elizabeth R. Moberly, *Psychogenesis: The Early Development of Gender Identity* (Worcester, U.K.: Billing & Sons, 1983), pp. 14-38.

[14]Comiskey, *Living Waters,* chapter seven.

[15]Ibid., chapter eight.

Chapter 7: Men at the Cross

[1]Larry Crabb, *The Silence of Adam: Becoming Men of Courage in a World of Chaos* (Grand Rapids, Mich.: Zondervan, 1995), pp. 101-2.

[2]Ibid., p. 12.

[3]Alan P. Medinger, *Growth into Manhood: Resuming the Journey* (Colorado Springs, Colo.: WaterBrook, 2000), pp. 135-38.

[4]Mike Bickle, *The Pleasures of Loving God* (Lake Mary, Fla.: Creation House, 2000), p. 47.

[5]Quoted in Jack Balswick, *Men at the Crossroads: Beyond Traditional Roles and Modern Options* (Downers Grove, Ill.: InterVarsity Press, 1992), p. 49.

[6]John Paul II, *The Theology of the Body: Human Love in the Divine Plan* (Boston: Pauline, 1997), p. 460.

Chapter 8: Women at the Cross

[1]Quoted in Karl Stern, *The Flight from Woman* (New York: Paragon, 1985), p. 26.

[2]John Paul II, *The Theology of the Body: Human Love in the Divine Plan* (Boston: Pauline, 1997), p. 469.

[3]Ibid., p. 485.

[4]Victor Hugo, *Les Misérables* (Hertfordshire, U.K.: Wordsworth, 1994), 2:631.

[5]John Paul II, *Theology of the Body,* p. 457.

[6]Stern, *Flight from Woman,* p. 17.

[7]Quoted in Leanne Payne, *Pastoral Care Ministries Newsletter,* spring 1989, p. 6.

[8]Hugo, *Les Misérables,* 2: 813.

[9]John Paul II, *Theology of the Body,* p. 457.

[10]Ibid., p. 465.

[11]Ibid., p. 467.

Chapter 9: Homosexuality and the Cross

[1]Quoted in Lorraine Kisley, ed., *Ordinary Graces: Christian Teachings on the Interior Life* (New York: Bell Tower, 2000), p. 61.

[2]Leanne Payne, *The Broken Image: Restoring Personal Wholeness Through Healing Prayer* (Westchester, Ill.: Crossway, 1981), p. 139.

[3]Thomas E. Schmidt, *Straight and Narrow? Compassion and Clarity in the Homosexuality Debate* (Downers Grove, Ill.: InterVarsity Press, 1995), p. 11.

[4]So stated Nada Stotland, head of the American Psychiatric Association's joint committee on public affairs, in "Therapy to Alter Gays," *Los Angeles Times,* December 12, 1998, p. A20.

[5]Robert L. Spitzer, "Commentary: Psychiatry and Homosexuality," *Wall Street Jour-*

nal, May 23, 2001, p. A26.

[6]Jeffrey Burke Satinover, *Homosexuality and the Politics of Truth* (Grand Rapids, Mich.: Baker, 1996), p. 136.

[7]Schmidt, *Straight and Narrow?* pp. 131-32.

[8]Anonymous letter to the editor, *Cornerstone Magazine* 20, no. 95 (1991).

[9]Norvene Vest, *No Moment Too Small: Rhythms of Silence, Prayer, and Holy Reading* (Kalamazoo, Mich.: Cistercian, 1994), pp. 120-21.

[10]Karl Rahner, quoted in Kisley, *Ordinary Graces,* p. 69.

[11]Ibid., p. 69.

[12]Dallas Willard, *The Divine Conspiracy: Rediscovering Our Hidden Life in God* (San Francisco: HarperSanFrancisco, 1998), p. 342.

[13]Vincent Van Gogh, *The Letters of Vincent Van Gogh,* ed. Mark Roskill (Hammersmith, U.K.: Flamingo, 2000), p. 295.

Chapter 10: The Church at the Cross

[1]Ray Anderson, *On Being Human: Essays in Theological Anthropology* (Grand Rapids, Mich.: Eerdmans, 1982), p. 183.